W9-CNZ-459

A MARRIAGE JOURNAL

SHARE YOUR HEART AND UNDERSTAND THEIRS

Navigator's COUNCIL

CONNECT, COMMUNICATE AND GROW IN
LOVE THROUGH 6 WEEKLY QUESTIONS

Jeremy & Audrey Roloff

A BEATING50PERCENT RESOURCE

Copyright © 2016

Beating 50 Percent LLC

All rights reserved. No portion of this book may be reproduced, distrib-
uted, or transmitted in any form or by any means, including photocopy-
ing, recording, or other electronic or mechanical methods, except for
the use of brief quotations in book reviews or articles, without the prior
written permission of the author.

ISBN-10:0-9978240-2-6
ISBN-13:978-0-9978240-2-5

Book Website: NavigatorsCouncil.com

Printed in U.S.A

W1 —————————— JOY	W27 —————————— PLAY
W2 —————————— COVENANT	W28 —————————— RHYTHM
W3 —————————— LOVE	W29 —————————— COMMUNITY
W4 —————————— PRIORITIZE	W30 —————————— ROMANCE
W5 —————————— BOUNDARIES	W31 —————————— PATIENCE
W6 —————————— ONENESS	W32 —————————— TEAMMATE
W7 —————————— TRUST	W33 —————————— PROTECT
W8 —————————— COMMUNICATE	W34 —————————— INTEGRITY
W9 —————————— COMPASSION	W35 —————————— RECONCILE
W10 —————————— REPENT	W36 —————————— HONESTY
W11 —————————— DREAM	W37 —————————— INTIMACY
W12 —————————— FORGIVE	W38 —————————— VISION
W13 —————————— SERVE	W39 —————————— CONNECT
W14 —————————— AFFIRM	W40 —————————— SPONTANEITY
W15 —————————— LEARN	W41 —————————— APPRECIATE
W16 —————————— PRAY	W42 —————————— HOPE
W17 —————————— ALWAYS MORE	W43 —————————— HONOR
W18 —————————— JOURNEY	W44 —————————— CHANGE
W19 —————————— ENCOURAGE	W45 —————————— EXPECTATIONS
W20 —————————— PURSUIT	W46 —————————— CONFLICT
W21 —————————— SACRIFICE	W47 —————————— SEEK
W22 —————————— SHARE	W48 —————————— CELEBRATE
W23 —————————— TRUTH	W49 —————————— FRIENDSHIP
W24 —————————— HUMILITY	W50 —————————— LISTEN
W25 —————————— SEX	W51 —————————— UNIQUE
W26 —————————— STEWARDSHIP	W52 —————————— REFLECT

FOREWORD

On June 20, 1998, my wife Jamie and I tied the knot. Our conception of "I do" turned out to be much different than we initially made it out to be. We quickly learned that marriage is work. We can either make deposits proactively, or frantically work reactively after everything has gone sideways. A few years in, we felt like ships in the night. Emotional deposits, significant conversations, dreams, goals, and romance seemed to have taken a dip in priority as work, kids, and activities dominated our schedule. There was a craving for significance and purpose, but we didn't have a resource to feed the desire. After much prayer, frustration, and conversation, we landed on five simple questions to ask one another every week. This process revolutionized our marriage, intimacy, and partnership. Our dream was to share these questions with others, but the project never seemed to get off the ground...

Enter Jeremy and Audrey. During their pre-marital counseling with us, we shared our little "Marriage Journal" with them. Immediately they fell in love with the concept of creating time and space to ask significant questions, communicate how they could serve one another, pray, and share their joys and hurts. They used the journal and, like Jeremy and Audrey always do, began to add their creative ideas, transforming our simple questions into a beautiful resource that takes marriages to greater depths of intimacy and purpose. Their Navigator's Council has the opportunity to be the greatest proactive deposit you ever make in your marriage. As you engage with this journal, emotional deposits will build-up and strengthen your trust, teamwork, and joy of simply being with one another.

Jeremy and Audrey model a passionate and purposeful marriage. This journal may be one of the greatest gifts your marriage has ever received. Our challenge: receive it. Open the gift! Try it faithfully for eight weeks, then ask yourselves this question: "are we better off as a couple?" Use Navigator's Council and receive the blessing of purposeful time together.

We are 18 years into marriage, have counseled over 60 couples, and believe this is the BEST resource for any couple who believes there is always more for their marriage. Don't settle! Choose one another. Start today.

In Him,
Chris and Jamie Herb

WHAT IS NAVIGATOR'S COUNCIL?

Navigator's Council is an interactive marriage journal featuring weekly questions to help you communicate, connect and grow in love.

The foundation of the journal is six weekly questions that you will ask each other, and then record your answers in the journaling section provided. The questions are designed to facilitate healthy communication on important topics.

Each week also includes a short devotional and a weeklong calendar. The devotionals will cultivate meaningful conversations, while also encouraging and challenging your marriage. The calendar is designed to help you set clear expectations for the week, and make sure you and your spouse are on the same page.

We are overjoyed that you are taking on this commitment as a step towards a better than average marriage, a marriage that is *Beating50Percent*. We hope that this practice is something you choose to commit to year after year.

*We named this journal Navigator's Council because it is a weekly council, that will help you navigate your marriage.

HOW TO USE THIS JOURNAL

1. Select one day of the week that works best for you and your spouse to consistently commit to your Navigator's Council.

2. Each week, start your Navigator's Council by reading a short devotional together and filling out your calendar for the week.

3. Flip to the next page and begin asking/answering the questions. Indicate whose answers are whose by writing each others names under each question, followed by your answers. Take turns every other week being the one to record the answers.

4. When you have completed all the questions, end your Navigator's Council each week in prayer. Don't forget to pray over the specific requests that were discussed in question six.

5. Repeat on the same day every week for a year.

6. Once you've completed this Navigator's Council journal, make sure you order a new journal so that you can continue recording the growth of your love year after year.

WHAT IS BEATING50PERCENT?

Beating50Percent is a community, ministry, blog, and resource for couples seeking to have, thriving, fulfilling, and better than average marriages. We are stubbornly confident that there are still people in pursuit of covenant marriages; marriages that are undividedly devoted, completely committed, persistently selfless, God-centered, joy-filled, and love-based. Our mission at *Beating50Percent* is to revive covenant marriages and inspire couples to give **more** than average to their spouses.

Our mission was inspired in part, by a photo that we saw in an old antique shop of an elderly couple holding each other close. Under the photo it read, "*Back in our day, when something broke, you fixed it instead of throwing it away.*" We found ourselves awestruck at the truth of the statement. When our grandparents were growing up, if their car, bike, sink, dress, bed, marriage or radio broke, they fixed it. Nowadays, most people wouldn't even know how to fix those things even if they wanted to. More than that, most people don't want to because they don't need to. If it breaks, they can just buy a new one, or a better one. Seemingly, nothing is irreplaceable, and unfortunately the same concept has translated to marriages. If it breaks, just get a new one.

Beating50percent aims to extinguish this perspective that marriages are unfixable. We hope to encourage couples to view their marriage as a covenant, an unbreakable union. We aspire to inspire husbands and wives to always give more than 50% effort to their spouses. We hope that through our blogs, posts, videos, and books, you will be compelled to relentlessly give more, serve more, learn more, play more, seek more, and love more... *always more*, in your marriages.

A LETTER FROM US

As we have reflected on our past entries, we smile at what this journal has prevented us from, and the standard it has held us to.

Navigator's Council is a call to reconciliation, a burning away of bitterness, and a revelation of truth. It has protected our marriage from sin, hurt, lies, attack, and poor communication.

Our prayer for you is that this Navigator's Council journal would do all of that and *more* for your marriage. We hope that someday you will have a bookshelf full of Navigator's Council journals that have strengthened and recorded the growth of your love.

Whether you are newlywed, or you've been married for 30 years, we believe our Navigator's Council journal will transform your marriage and deepen your oneness. We are stoked that you are making this commitment as a step toward a better than average marriage.

Under the Mercy,
Jeremy & Audrey Roloff

Joy

Joy is not circumstantial. In Christ, we ALWAYS have access to MORE joy. Is your marriage marked by joy?

Each week during our Navigator's Council, we (and now you) start by asking each other this simple question:

"What brought you JOY this week?"

This question brings us to a place of thanksgiving and praise to God. Maybe it's just me, but I don't think I'm alone when I say that, as women, we are often more inclined to remember what our husbands did wrong last week, than we are able to recite what brought them joy! Let's be women who know our husbands' joys more than their faults. Let's be women who are quick to share what brought us joy with a thankful heart.

Joy is always given, never grasped. Christ fills us up with more and *more* joy, as we continue to trust His ways and follow them. The Message version of John 15:11 says, "I've told you these things for a purpose: that my joy might be your joy, and your joy **wholly** mature." (MSG)

Wholly mature joy requires wholly surrendered trust. Is there a circumstance in your life or area in your relationship in which you are not trusting God in? Do not let a lack of trust, rob you of the infinite joy that is offered to you.

I've heard it asked, *"Isn't joy worth the effort of trust?"*

- Audrey

Calendar

_____ / / _____

Mon.	Tue.
Wed.	Thur.
Fri.	Sat.
Sun.	Other:

Notes

Navigators

1. What brought you joy this week?

2. What is something that was hard this week?

3. What is one specific thing I can do for you this week?

4. Is there any unconfessed sin, conflict, or hurt that we need to resolve and/or seek forgiveness for?

5. What is a dream, craving, or desire that has been on the forefront of your mind?

6. How can I pray for you this week?

Love

"...Love one another. As I have loved you, so you must love one another. By this everyone will know that you are my disciples, if you love one another." John 13:34-35 (NIV)

Love is not a feeling; it's a sacrifice, a verb, a commitment, and a daily choice. Your love for your spouse is how others will see Christ in you (Ephesians 5:33). God uses our marriages to advertise the Gospel. We live in a world where it is more common for people to rebuke or neglect the teachings of Jesus, rather than follow them. I wonder how much of this is a result of the increasing ugliness within Christian marriages? What if our marriages were a better reflection of the love of Christ? Think of how much more we could make the love of Christ known if we better reflected this love in our marriages!

As you grow to love Christ more, you are able to love your spouse *more*. It is only by His unending love that we have the capacity to love without bounds - to *always* love *more*. 1 John 4:7-8 says, "...let us love one another, for love comes from God. Everyone who loves has been born of God and knows God. Whoever does not love does not know God, because God is love." (NIV)

"In any relationship, there will be frightening spells in which your feelings of love dry up. And when that happens, you must remember that the essence of marriage is that it is a covenant, a commitment, a promise of future love. So what do you do? You do the acts of love, despite your lack of feeling. You may not feel tender, sympathetic, and eager to please, but in your actions you must BE tender, understanding, forgiving and helpful. And, if you do that, as time goes on you will not only get through the dry spells, but they will become less frequent and deep, and you will become more constant in your feelings. This is what can happen if you decide to love." – Timothy Keller

- Audrey

Calendar

_____ / / _____

Mon.	**Tue.**
Wed.	**Thur.**
Fri.	**Sat.**
Sun.	**Other:**

Notes

_____

_____

_____

_____

_____

_____

_____

_____

_____

_____

Navigators

1. What brought you joy this week?

2. What is something that was hard this week?

3. What is one specific thing I can do for you this week?

4. Is there any unconfessed sin, conflict, or hurt that we need to resolve and/or seek forgiveness for?

5. What is a dream, craving, or desire that has been on the forefront of your mind?

6. How can I pray for you this week?

Prioritize

Your priorities reveal where you are dedicating your efforts. Is your husband/wife your number one priority, only second to your relationship with Christ?

Did you answer the question above, "yes?" Now ask yourself, "Are my actions *proving* that my husband/wife is my priority?"

Sometimes we fall into habits and routines that don't truly reflect what is most important to us. We get lazy. We fall into the trap of pursuing what's *easy* over what's *valuable*.

Here are a few ways Audrey and I intentionally prioritize each other:

Unhindered time – We try our best to create time and space each week where we can get away (or stay in) and connect with each other through quality time. For example, taking a Sabbath, going out to dinner, cooking a meal, playing a game, or going for an evening walk.

By putting down our phones – We have created parameters around our digital consumption. For example, a "no phone zone," or a designated time to *turn off* our phones (can you believe it!?!?) and put them in a drawer for the night.

Through the little things – Consistent actions of love that say, "I love you, I prioritize you, and you are worth it." For example, notes on the bathroom mirror, a surprise gift, a hug or kiss, or even just saying "thank you."

The fact that you have committed to Navigator's Council is an immense step towards prioritizing your marriage (high-five!).

What are some other ways you demonstrate that your husband/wife is your priority through your actions?

- Jeremy

Calendar

_____ / / _____

Mon.	**Tue**.
Wed.	**Thur**.
Fri.	**Sat**.
Sun.	Other:

Notes

_____
_____
_____
_____
_____
_____
_____
_____
_____

Navigators

1. What brought you joy this week?

2. What is something that was hard this week?

3. What is one specific thing I can do for you this week?

4. Is there any unconfessed sin, conflict, or hurt that we need to resolve and/or seek forgiveness for?

5. What is a dream, craving, or desire that has been on the fore-front of your mind?

6. How can I pray for you this week?

MONTHLY QUESTIONS

☐ How are we stewarding our finances?

☐ How is our sex life?

Boundaries

"While many dynamics go into producing and maintaining love, over and over again one issue is at the top of the list: boundaries. When boundaries are not established in the beginning of a marriage, or when they break down, marriages break down as well.... For this intimacy to develop and grow, there must be boundaries." - *Boundaries in Marriage* by Henry Cloud and John Townsend

Before we were married, Jer and I were encouraged by our pre-marital counselors to set some boundaries for our marriage. We like to refer to them as our "black and whites for marriage," or put another way, the things we will say *yes* or *no* to, regardless of circumstances.

A ski boundary line, a railing on a bridge, a divider in a freeway, directions on the back of a medication, these things are not set in place to hinder you, they are set in place to protect and preserve you. The same is true with boundaries in your marriage.

Here are a few of our boundaries for marriage: Never talk bad about your spouse, no secrets, eliminate "you never" and "you always" from your vocabulary, don't withhold sex, don't be alone with the opposite sex, "no phone zones" in your house/times of day, don't fight in public, don't drink while trying to resolve an issue or conflict, back each other up/praise each other in public, don't compare your marriage to someone else's, don't disagree/correct each other in public, don't go to bed angry, don't vent to friends, family, or social media about marriage conflict, don't ever physically fight, and never sleep on the couch or in a different bed because you're mad.

Do you have a list of "black and whites" for your marriage?
If not, consider creating your own list of boundaries together. Write them down.

- Audrey

Calendar

_____ / / _____

Mon.	**Tue.**
Wed.	**Thur.**
Fri.	**Sat.**
Sun.	Other:

Notes

_____
_____
_____
_____
_____
_____
_____
_____
_____
_____

Navigators

1. What brought you joy this week?

2. What is something that was hard this week?

3. What is one specific thing I can do for you this week?

4. Is there any unconfessed sin, conflict, or hurt that we need to resolve and/or seek forgiveness for?

5. What is a dream, craving, or desire that has been on the forefront of your mind?

6. How can I pray for you this week?

Oneness

"That is why a man leaves his father and mother and is united to his wife, and they **become one flesh.**" Genesis 2:24 (NIV)

Oneness is both a moment *and* a daily choice. Think of it this way, we become one with Christ in a moment (salvation/baptism Mark 16:16) **and** we become one with Christ every day as we choose to follow Him through the everyday choices. Oneness, much like our salvation, is not something that can be thrown away. Marriage is a covenant, not a contract. A covenant is *for better* or *for worse*. Oneness is both a *truth* about our marriage and a *practice* -- something we get to live out daily. In the same way, we become one with our spouse on our wedding day, *and* we continue to become one with them every day through choices that say "less me, more we." Becoming one means replacing "I, me, mine" with "We, us, and ours." For example, our house, our kids, and our bank account.

However, the "we" statements should not stop with material possessions. In our house, it's my job to take out the trash. Sometimes, I forget... and Audrey gets frustrated, and points out my fault. Likewise, I get frustrated with Audrey when we are late going somewhere because she took too long getting ready. I blame our tardiness on her. We've been working on turning these types of situations from blame shifting into "*we* shifting." So instead of Audrey saying, "Jer you forgot to take out the trash," she says, "Jer, *we* forgot to take out the trash." And instead of me saying, "Auj was running late," I say, "*We* are running late." It would be the same if Audrey got cancer. I wouldn't say that *Audrey* has cancer, but rather, *we* have cancer. Becoming one in our faults and hardships has helped us remember we are on the same team, and prevented defensiveness.

Think of an example in your marriage of how you can turn blame shifting into "*we* shifting."

- Jeremy

Calendar

_____ / / _____

Mon.	**Tue.**
Wed.	**Thur.**
Fri.	**Sat.**
Sun.	Other:

Notes

_____

_____
_____
_____
_____
_____
_____
_____
_____
_____
_____

Navigators

1. What brought you joy this week?

2. What is something that was hard this week?

3. What is one specific thing I can do for you this week?

4. Is there any unconfessed sin, conflict, or hurt that
    we need to resolve and/or seek forgiveness for?

5. What is a dream, craving, or desire that has been on the fore-
    front of your mind?

6. How can I pray for you this week?

Trust

"Trust in and rely confidently on the Lord with all your heart And do not rely on your own insight or understanding…" Proverbs 3:5 (AMP)

We cannot have a healthy relationship with Christ if we do not trust Him, and we cannot have a healthy relationship with our spouse, if we do not trust him/her. Trust is a catalyst to transformation, and we serve a God that is in the business of transforming hearts, not just inspiring thoughts and actions.

Withholding trust from your spouse will eventually hurt much more than giving it freely. Christ wants trust to be at the center of our relationship with Him, *and* at the center our relationship with our husband or wife. Trust has the beautiful ability to defeat a multitude of insecurities and doubts. When you trust someone, you are encased in emotional security and safety. Relationships that are built on trust create room for honesty and breed healing and growth. Building trust, in God and your spouse, requires effort and sacrifice – but the peace that follows is worth the effort of sacrifice.

Proverbs 31:11 says, "The heart of her husband trusts in her, and he will have no lack of gain." (ESV)

One of my broken record sayings is: *God's past faithfulness demands our present **TRUST**.* Likewise, your husband or wife's past faithfulness demands your present trust. Trust them *more* through your actions this week!

"...in quietness and TRUST is your strength." Isaiah 30:15 (NIV)

*If there is sin or hurt in your relationship that is preventing the work of trust from transforming your marriage, seek forgiveness and reconciliation this week.

- Audrey

Calendar

_____ / _____ / _____

Mon.	Tue.
Wed.	Thur.
Fri.	Sat.
Sun.	Other:

Notes

Navigator's

1. What brought you joy this week?

2. What is something that was hard this week?

3. What is one specific thing I can do for you this week?

4. Is there any unconfessed sin, conflict, or hurt that we need to resolve and/or seek forgiveness for?

5. What is a dream, craving, or desire that has been on the fore-front of your mind?

6. How can I pray for you this week?

Communicate

What is the first marriage advice you received?

I'm going to guess it was something along the lines of… "communicate, communicate, communicate."

Getting to know someone requires *communication*. It's how we fall in love, it's how we understand their heart, and it's how we resolve issues that arise, share dreams, and discuss our needs.

The less Audrey and I communicate, the more we end up fighting. When we don't communicate, we are not on the same page and often end up feeling misunderstood. This is especially true when we don't lay out our expectations. It leaves room for confusion, frustration, and disappointment. Frustration comes from confusion, while clarity comes from *communication.*

Communication is an essential part of staying connected, managing expectations, meeting needs, knowing what to pray for, making decisions, reconciling, learning, understanding, growing, serving, and loving well.

Communication is what this journal is all about! Navigator's Council was designed to create time and space for a "good time to talk about it." Communication is a discipline that we must learn to prioritize in our marriage. Without the discipline of communication, we are left to assume. Navigator's Council doesn't leave room for assumptions. It turns communicating well, into loving well.

We hope and pray that this journal has been, and will be, an effective tool for connectivity and communication in your marriage.

- Jeremy

Calendar

_____ / ___ / _____

Mon.	**Tue.**
Wed.	**Thur.**
Fri.	**Sat.**
Sun.	Other:

Notes
_____
_____
_____
_____
_____
_____
_____
_____
_____
_____

Navigators

1. What brought you joy this week?

2. What is something that was hard this week?

3. What is one specific thing I can do for you this week?

4. Is there any unconfessed sin, conflict, or hurt that we need to resolve and/or seek forgiveness for?

5. What is a dream, craving, or desire that has been on the fore-front of your mind?

6. How can I pray for you this week?

MONTHLY QUESTIONS

☐ How are we stewarding our finances?

☐ How is our sex life?

Compassion

Put yourself in your spouse's shoes this week. For some of us, empathizing does not come easy, but we must learn it in order to love compassionately. Colossians 3:12 says, "...as those who have been chosen of God, holy and beloved, put on a heart of *compassion*, kindness, humility, gentleness and patience..." (NASB)

Be compassionately curious before you're carelessly critical. We are most critical of the people we spend the most time with. This is because our humanness is often bent toward correcting others, rather than humbling ourselves. Maybe today you criticized your husband or wife for something he or she did. I probably did... I am often quick to point out what Jeremy did or said that was wrong rather than compassionately asking a question about his words/actions that would facilitate a productive conversation.

For example, let's say I felt like Jeremy wasn't listening to me. My first reaction would probably be something like, "You never listen!" This critical and offensive approach to conflict will only initiate arguments rather than reconcile issues. Instead, I should have asked him a "compassionately curious" question. The best way to do this would have been to ask a question like this, "Hey babe, do you feel like I let you talk when we are having a discussion or am I sometimes overbearing?" This kind of question comes from a place of humility rather than offensiveness. If we are going to initiate conversations with our husbands and wives that *may* come across as critical, we must be willing to start from a place of humility.

We must be more concerned with progress, than proving a point. Compassionate curiosity - *without* an agenda - has the power to foster intimacy, increase communication, stimulate growth, heal wounds, breed peace, and deepen love. **How can you be more compassionately curious in your relationship this week?**

- Audrey

Calendar

_____ / / _____

Mon.	**Tue.**
Wed.	**Thur.**
Fri.	**Sat.**
Sun.	Other:

Notes

Navigators

1. What brought you joy this week?

2. What is something that was hard this week?

3. What is one specific thing I can do for you this week?

4.   Is there any unconfessed sin, conflict, or hurt that we need to resolve and/or seek forgiveness for?

5.   What is a dream, craving, or desire that has been on the fore-front of your mind?

6.   How can I pray for you this week?

Repent

Saying "sorry" for the same thing over and over again is a clear indication that you are not actually sorry. **A true apology is changed behavior**. Scripture calls it *repentance*. To "repent" means to turn away from.

When we hurt our spouse, or have an evil addiction or a bad habit we can't seem to break, a sorry can be an emotional Band-Aid or hollow words that are supposed to imply changed behavior. When that Band-Aid falls off and you find yourself saying sorry again for the exact same thing, it begs the question: are you truly sorry?

We show how much we value things by how we treat them. If you own a house, you demonstrate how much you value it through cleaning it, updating it, maintaining it, decorating it, and taking good care of it. In the same way, we prove how much we value our spouses by how we treat them. **Love is a verb.** We can say a thousand "*I love you's*" and "*I'm sorry's,*" but our actions will prove what and who we truly love, whether it be our spouse or ourselves.

This is not to omit grace, but let's not use grace as a crutch for our hurtful actions, destructive addictions, or sinful behaviors.

Is your marriage marked by repentance? Or are you continuing to walk in the same sin sorry after sorry? The Bible says that we are victors in Christ. Through Jesus, we are called to repent, turn away from our selfish behaviors, and walk in victorious glory! (Romans 8:37)

Is there something in your marriage that you are constantly apologizing for? Be willing to repent, embrace forgiveness, and walk in in freedom! Romans 6:11 says, "Even so consider yourselves to be dead to sin, but alive to God in Christ Jesus." (NASB)

- Jeremy

Calendar

_____ / / _____

Mon.	**Tue**.
Wed.	**Thur**.
Fri.	**Sat**.
Sun.	**Other:**

Notes

Navigators

1. What brought you joy this week?

2. What is something that was hard this week?

3. What is one specific thing I can do for you this week?

4. Is there any unconfessed sin, conflict, or hurt that we need to resolve and/or seek forgiveness for?

5. What is a dream, craving, or desire that has been on the fore-front of your mind?

6. How can I pray for you this week?

Dream

"Delight yourself in the Lord, and he will give you the desires of your heart." Psalm 37:4 (ESV)

Oh how I hope you dream big dreams with your spouse!

Yes, hold them loosely, but don't be afraid to **pray big prayers!**

Do you trust in a God who desires to give you good gifts?

Marriage is one of the greatest gifts that God has given us, and He created it to be good (Genesis 2:18). Set high hopes for your marriage and be confident that the Lord wants your marriage to thrive.

Ephesians 3:20 says, "Now to him who is able to do **immeasurably more** than all we ask or imagine, according to his power that is at work in us." (ESV) His power is at work in your marriage, and He wants your marriage to be **immeasurably more** than you could ever ask or imagine. You can do ALL THINGS through Christ who strengthens you! (Philippians 4:13)

Ask God to align your dreams with His heart and His purposes. Then believe the scripture that says, "ask and it will be given to you." (Matthew 7:7) NIV

The Message puts it this way, "He said, 'That's what I mean: Risk your life and get more than you ever dreamed of. Play it safe and end up holding a bag..." Luke 19:26 (MSG)

Dream together, and dream big!

- Audrey

Calendar

_____ / _____ / _____

Mon.	Tue.
Wed.	**Thur.**
Fri.	**Sat.**
Sun.	**Other:** Spend some time dreaming together this week!

Notes

Navigators

1. What brought you joy this week?

2. What is something that was hard this week?

3. What is one specific thing I can do for you this week?

4. Is there any unconfessed sin, conflict, or hurt that we need to resolve and/or seek forgiveness for?

5. What is a dream, craving, or desire that has been on the forefront of your mind?

6. How can I pray for you this week?

Forgive

Forgiveness. I think we can all agree on how difficult this can be.

The Bible gives us clear instructions in regards to forgiveness. We cannot receive forgiveness unless we are willing to forgive (Matthew 6:14-15; Mark 11:25).

Colossians 3:13 says "... if one has a complaint against another, forgiving each other; as the Lord has forgiven you, so you also must forgive." (ESV) God offers us complete forgiveness, so we are likewise called to forgive. We forgive because we are commanded to do so. We also forgive because it's very difficult to love someone if you are harboring bitterness toward him or her. Grudges, resentment, and bitterness create cancerous conditions in relationships. They only lead to conflict and strife. As Josh McDowell puts it, **"Forgiveness is the oil of relationships."**

Unforgiveness is a form of keeping score against one another when we're supposed to be on the same team! There will always be wrongdoings committed against us. In Matthew 18:22, Peter asks Jesus how we are to forgive. Jesus answered, "I do not say to you, up to seven times, but up to seventy times seven." (NKJV) What He meant was, *tirelessly.* Without a heart of forgiveness, a healthy relationship is not possible. Love keeps no records of wrongs. (1 Corinthians 13:5)

"Until you let your past die, it will not let your future live" - Jimmy Evans

If you are harboring bitterness from unforgiveness, use question number four in your Navigator's Council this week, to begin the conversation, and start the healing process.

- Jeremy

Calendar

_____ / _____ / _____

Mon.	**Tue.**
Wed.	**Thur.**
Fri.	**Sat.**
Sun.	Other:

Notes

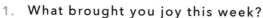

Navigator's

1. What brought you joy this week?

2. What is something that was hard this week?

3. What is one specific thing I can do for you this week?

4. Is there any unconfessed sin, conflict, or hurt that we need to resolve and/or seek forgiveness for?

5. What is a dream, craving, or desire that has been on the fore-
   front of your mind?

6. How can I pray for you this week?

MONTHLY QUESTIONS

☐ How are we stewarding our finances?

☐ How is our sex life?

Serve

Galatians 5:13 says, "You, my brothers and sisters, were called to be free. But do not use your freedom to indulge the flesh; rather, _serve_ one another humbly in love." (NIV)

This whole "If you do this, I will do that" attitude toward your spouse has the potential to ruin your marriage. It's not the way God designed it to be.

Healthy relationships are marked by _two givers_, serving one another with grace, compassion, knowledge, and love. God didn't say to treat your spouse with respect and serve them only if they do so in return... that's conditional love. We are called to love our spouses by serving them with humility. We show our love by counting others needs and wants as more important than our own (Philippians 2:4).

Romans 12:10 says, "Love one another with brotherly affection. Outdo one another in showing honor." (ESV)

Spend some extra time on question number three this week. Be honest about one specific thing your spouse can do for you.

May you "outdo one another in showing honor" this week. May you serve more.

- Audrey

Calendar

_____ / / _____

Mon.	**Tue.**
Wed.	**Thur.**
Fri.	**Sat.**
Sun.	**Other:** Think of one creative way you can serve your spouse this week.

Notes

_____
_____
_____
_____
_____
_____
_____
_____
_____
_____

Navigators

1. What brought you joy this week?

2. What is something that was hard this week?

3. What is one specific thing I can do for you this week?

4. Is there any unconfessed sin, conflict, or hurt that we need to resolve and/or seek forgiveness for?

5. What is a dream, craving, or desire that has been on the forefront of your mind?

6. How can I pray for you this week?

Affirm

Affirmation unlocks adoration.

Affirming is a great way of supporting. When we affirm our spouses, we let them know that we believe in them, we value them, we support them, and that we are for them, one hundred percent. 1 Corinthians 15:58 says, "... Always give yourselves fully to the work of the Lord, because you know that your labor in the Lord is not in vain." (NIV) Our spouses need us to affirm them that whatever they are working on or working towards is not in vain.

We need to be affirming each other in public *and* in private. As we do life with our spouses, it's important to encourage and affirm them because often times they don't notice their own improvement. Remember, an affirming word from you will always mean more than one from someone else.

In our second year of marriage, I had a hard time remembering to affirm Audrey. She knew I loved her, supported her, and was for her, but just knowing is not enough. I needed to show her. I came to this realization through our Navigator's Council.

One week, during our Navigator's Council, I learned that Audrey was feeling a little neglected and was needing more words of affirmation from me. So, for her birthday, I bought her a "gratitude jar." Every day I began telling her something that I appreciate or love about her. Then I would write it down and put it in the jar. Audrey *loved* it and felt encouraged, uplifted, and supported. It also softened my heart even more towards her as I watched the practice of affirmation take effect.

I encourage you to be your spouse's biggest fan. A kind word from you will always mean the most, because you know him or her the best. Be an affirmer.

- Jeremy

Calendar

_____ / / _____

Mon.	Tue.
Wed.	**Thur.**
Fri.	**Sat.**
Sun.	**Other:**

Notes

_____

_____

_____

_____

_____

_____

_____

_____

_____

_____

Navigator's

1. What brought you joy this week?

2. What is something that was hard this week?

3. What is one specific thing I can do for you this week?

4. Is there any unconfessed sin, conflict, or hurt that
    we need to resolve and/or seek forgiveness for?

5. What is a dream, craving, or desire that has been on the fore-
    front of your mind?

6. How can I pray for you this week?

Learn

Be a student of your spouse. Never stop seeking to learn and understand them. Intentionally pay attention to their habits, good and bad, so that you are equipped to love them well, no matter the circumstance.

In regards to learning and understanding our spouses, 1 Peter 3:7 says that we are to, "dwell with them according to knowledge." (KJV) Meaning, we are to love our spouses according to knowledge. In order to acquire knowledge, we must be willing to keep learning *more*.

We must seek to discover more of who our spouses are, what they like, their past, their day-to-day, their struggles, their triumphs, their fears, their hopes, and their dreams. Ask questions. Be curious. Don't stop getting to know your spouse!

On your 10-year wedding anniversary, your spouse will mostly likely not be the same person that you said, "I do" to, but this should be something that excites you! As Jeremy put it in his wedding vows to me, "I promise to pursue the new you every year."

At the core, every single human on the planet has a desire to be loved and known, but we cannot know and love each other well without learning about each other. Learning turns knowing more into loving more. **ALWAYS** loving, **MORE** and more.

One of the ways you can learn more about your spouse is through Navigator's Council each week. Take advantage of the opportunity to discover new things about your spouse and new ways to creatively and specifically love him or her well.

- Audrey

Calendar

_____ / / _____

Mon.	Tue.
Wed.	**Thur.**
Fri.	**Sat.**
Sun.	Other:

Notes

_____

_____

_____

_____

_____

_____

_____

_____

_____

_____

Navigators

1. What brought you joy this week?

2. What is something that was hard this week?

3. What is one specific thing I can do for you this week?

Council

4. Is there any unconfessed sin, conflict, or hurt that
    we need to resolve and/or seek forgiveness for?

5. What is a dream, craving, or desire that has been on the fore-
    front of your mind?

6. How can I pray for you this week?

Pray

Husband! Are you leading your family in prayer? How often do you pray with your wife? How often are you praying protection over her and your family?

Husbands, we need to be the initiators. Husbands, we need to lead the charge and be praying *for, over* and *with* our wives.

We need to be gentle in person, but unbridled in prayer.

Likewise, wives, have you prayed about it more than you've talked about it? It's not your job to change your spouse's heart. It's God's job to change hearts - it's your job to pray. Through prayer, we might even realize that perhaps our own heart is the one in need of changing.

Scripture tells us to "ask and it will be given" (Matthew 7:7). Are you quick to ask God in prayer to change your spouse's heart, or are you trying to change them yourself?

Without Him we can't, and without us He won't. What this means is, God is our strength and ability to do anything, but we have a job to do as well. We need to ask Him - in **prayer.**

I encourage you to pray daily for your spouse. Seek out more opportunities to pray *over* her and **with** her. If you haven't ever prayed with your spouse before, let today mark the beginning. It might be awkward, it might be uncomfortable, you might not know what to pray for, or how to pray, but that's all ok with God. The more you do it, the easier it will be, and the more powerfully God will work in your life and your marriage. Jesus said that where two or three are gathered in my name, there I am with them (Matthew 18:20). Prayer it too powerful to be left out - it moves the hand of God.

- Jeremy

Calendar

_____ / _____ / _____

Mon.	**Tue.**
Wed.	**Thur.**
Fri.	**Sat.**
Sun.	Other:

Notes

Navigator's

1. What brought you joy this week?

2. What is something that was hard this week?

3. What is one specific thing I can do for you this week?

4. Is there any unconfessed sin, conflict, or hurt that we need to resolve and/or seek forgiveness for?

5. What is a dream, craving, or desire that has been on the fore-front of your mind?

6. How can I pray for you this week?

MONTHLY QUESTIONS

☐ How are we stewarding our finances?

☐ How is our sex life?

Always More

The meaning behind *"always more"* is part of the reason behind *Beating50Percent* - the name of our marriage mission and ministry.

Beating50Percent is about inspiring and encouraging couples to seek better than average marriages and to give *more* than fifty percent effort to their spouses. We hope that our mission will motivate you to relentlessly give more, serve more, learn more, play more, seek more, and love more... *always more*, in your marriage.

These words, *"always more,"* are a reminder that there is *always more* to look forward to, *more* than meets the eye, *more* to someone's story, *more* to be thankful for, *more* to give, *more* to unearth, *more* to learn, *more* fun to be had, *more* blessings to receive, *more* kindness to offer, *more* fruit to bear, *more* growth in faith, *more* peace to experience, *more* mercy to grant, *more* wisdom to gain, and *more* reason to love (Ephesians 3:20).

An excerpt from Audrey's wedding vows: "But I also write these words on my hand as a reminder that by Christ's strength, there are *always more* ways that I can serve you, *more* things that I can learn about you, *more* grace to grant you, *more* humility to have towards you, *more* support to offer you, *more* laughter to share with you, *more* children to give you, *more* adventure to seek with you, *more* passion to share with you, *more* faith to have in you, *more* places to go with you, *more* people to meet with you, *more* prayers to pray with you, *more* ways to worship with you, and *more* love to give to you."

What are some ways that you can seek *more* in your marriage? How can you give *more* to your spouse?

- Audrey

Calendar

_____ / / _____

Mon.	Tue.
Wed.	**Thur.**
Fri.	**Sat.**
Sun.	Other:

Notes

_____

_____
_____
_____
_____
_____
_____
_____
_____
_____

Navigators

1. What brought you joy this week?

2. What is something that was hard this week?

3. What is one specific thing I can do for you this week?

4. Is there any unconfessed sin, conflict, or hurt that we need to resolve and/or seek forgiveness for?

5. What is a dream, craving, or desire that has been on the fore-front of your mind?

6. How can I pray for you this week?

Journey

Good stories are journeys because they move you from place to place.

No wise traveler starts a journey without preparation. They prepare, plan, and manage their expectations. We're all en route towards a fun, intimate, encouraging, thriving, and healthy marriage. There will be flat tires, pot holes, and wrong turns along the way. But a wrong turn or flat tire does not define the journey; it only adds to the story. A wise traveler stays the course.

The journey towards a healthy and thriving marriage will take your *whole life*, *all* that you've got in you and *consistent* commitment to overcome obstacles. You can't build a story like this in a day or fix what may get broken overnight. Always remember that the breakdowns are pit stops, not destinations. For every rough spot there is a lesson to be learned, something to be realized, a habit to be changed, or a perspective to adopt. Don't let a circumstance define the status of your marriage, but rather define the circumstance by the posture of your attitude!

Be encouraged to know that as marriage travelers we are on a journey. The definition of traveling (or journey) is 'moving from one place to another.' If you do hit a rough patch in the road, don't compare it to someone else's smooth patch and don't compare their outsides with your insides.

Recognize that your marriage *is* a journey, so that you can plan to be a wise and prepared traveler.

– Jeremy

Calendar

_____ / / _____

Mon.	**Tue.**
Wed.	**Thur.**
Fri.	**Sat.**
Sun.	**Other:**

Notes

_____

_____

_____

_____

_____

_____

_____

_____

_____

_____

_____

Navigators

1. What brought you joy this week?

2. What is something that was hard this week?

3. What is one specific thing I can do for you this week?

4. Is there any unconfessed sin, conflict, or hurt that we need to resolve and/or seek forgiveness for?

5. What is a dream, craving, or desire that has been on the fore-front of your mind?

6. How can I pray for you this week?

Encourage

"Therefore encourage one another and build each other up, just as in fact you are doing." 1 Thessalonians 5:11 (NIV)

If your spouse's top love language is "words of affirmation," then learning how to encourage him or her well should be *especially* important to you. But, even if it's not their number one love language, we all still need "*words of affirmation*" to some degree.

Be your husband or wife's number one fan. Cheer them on, lift them up, and remind them of the truth about who they are and who they are becoming. This takes practice of course, but be willing to learn how to consistently and creatively encourage your spouse (Hebrews 10:24-25).

Jeremy and I give and receive encouragement in different ways. We had to learn how to encourage each other most effectively by asking questions and practicing different ways of encouraging each other.

Words are powerful. How you speak and what you say to your husband or wife *matters*. It's likely that you know your spouse better than anyone else does. You know what lies they are tempted to believe and what truths they need to be reminded of. You have the power to yank the lies from their life and permeate their mind and heart with refreshing, emboldening, and enlivening truth. Encouragement has a way of killing the lies of the enemy.

Here are a few ideas for encouraging your spouse this week:
Write them a love letter and address it to your home or their work, write a list of ten things you love about them on the bathroom mirror, write out a prayer for them and tape it to their car steering wheel, write out a list of ten words that describe their character and leave it on the kitchen counter, or send daily thank you notes via text.

- Audrey

Calendar

_____ / _____ / _____

Mon.	Tue.
Wed.	**Thur.**
Fri.	**Sat.**
Sun.	Other:

Notes

Navigators

1. What brought you joy this week?

2. What is something that was hard this week?

3. What is one specific thing I can do for you this week?

Council

4. Is there any unconfessed sin, conflict, or hurt that we need to resolve and/or seek forgiveness for?

5. What is a dream, craving, or desire that has been on the forefront of your mind?

6. How can I pray for you this week?

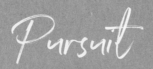

Pursuit

When I was in high school, I saw a car that completely transfixed me. I fell in love and *had* to have one…. I started researching, saving, and then Craigslisting, until I purchased my very own. However, my pursuit did not end at acquiring this new vehicle. That was not enough for me; I wanted more! I wanted to discover more about this car, study the ins and outs, and become an expert owner. So I began restoring it, joining clubs, going to coffee and car gatherings, etc. I'm sure some of you can relate.

I'll admit, this might be a silly story, but it demonstrates the kind of pursuit and continued investment that we are supposed to mimic in our marriage relationships. We should be constantly pursuing, learning, discovering, and loving our spouse more and *more*.

And yes, this is *much* easier said than done. Pursuit is difficult, fun, and absolutely vital to a healthy happy marriage.

This is where my story breaks down…. unlike a car, our spouses are constantly changing. There will always be a new version of them year after year that requires us to press into pursuit.

To stop pursuing Audrey year after year would be to intentionally fall out of love.

Scripture gives us very clear instructions on how we are to love and pursue our spouse "just as Christ loved the church." (Ephesians 5:25) Christ, in His pursuit of us gave His life. This is what pursuit is supposed to look like: creative, aggressive, complete, and persistent.

Keep on the pursuit! Remember, **to find and <u>still seek</u>, now that is love.**

- Jeremy

Calendar

_____ / / _____

Mon.	**Tue**.
Wed.	**Thur**.
Fri.	**Sat**.
Sun.	Other:

Notes

_____

_____

_____

_____

_____

_____

_____

_____

_____

_____

Navigators

1. What brought you joy this week?

2. What is something that was hard this week?

3. What is one specific thing I can do for you this week?

4. Is there any unconfessed sin, conflict, or hurt that we need to resolve and/or seek forgiveness for?

Council

5. What is a dream, craving, or desire that has been on the fore-
    front of your mind?

6. How can I pray for you this week?

MONTHLY QUESTIONS

☐ How are we stewarding our finances?

☐ How is our sex life?

Sacrifice

"The general human failing is to want what is right and important, but at the same time not to commit to the kind of life that will produce the action we know to be right and the condition we want to enjoy. We intend what is right, but we avoid the life that would make it reality." - Dallas Willard

This quote outlines the juxtaposition between what we want and what we are willing to give up to get there. We all want to have a thriving, loving, growing, and happy marriage, but are we willing to make the necessary *sacrifices* in order for that to be possible? Ephesians 5:25 teaches that our love for one another should be sacrificial. My deepest desire is to love Jeremy sacrificially, but unfortunately, like the Dallas Willard quote, *"I avoid the life that would make this a reality."* This juxtaposition is a fierce play-off between our deepest desires and our strongest desires. Our *deepest* desire might be to love our spouse sacrificially, but our strongest desire might be to do what is convenient, easy, pleasurable, and satisfying to ourselves in the moment. Deepest desires are those desires that transcend circumstances, while strongest desires are the desires that are reactionary and impulsive. In order to love sacrificially, *we must not let our strongest desires overcome our deepest desires.*

Our deepest desires are the ones that typically produce a lasting reward, while our strongest desires are fleeting and unfulfilling. Once we believe this to be true, we can start viewing *sacrifice* as an *investment* in our deepest desire, rather than a sunk cost. Stop avoiding sacrifice, and start willingly and eagerly embracing it. Sacrifice is one of the greatest investments you can make in your marriage and one of the greatest actions of love (1John 3:16). **What are some areas in your relationship where you have let your strongest desires overcome your deepest desires? What sacrifice do you need to view as an investment?**

- Audrey

Calendar

_____ / / _____

Mon.	Tue.
Wed.	**Thur.**
Fri.	**Sat.**
Sun.	**Other:**
	How are you going to prioritize intamacy this week?

Notes

_____
_____
_____
_____
_____
_____
_____
_____
_____

Navigators

1. What brought you joy this week?

2. What is something that was hard this week?

3. What is one specific thing I can do for you this week?

4. Is there any unconfessed sin, conflict, or hurt that we need to resolve and/or seek forgiveness for?

5. What is a dream, craving, or desire that has been on the forefront of your mind?

6. How can I pray for you this week?

Share

Audrey and I have a favorite book. I've read it once a year since the year I started dating Audrey. During my second year reading it, I read it out loud to Audrey. It's a true story, written by Sheldon Vanauken. The book is titled, *A Severe Mercy*. It's a beautiful love story between Sheldon and his lover, Davey. In the book they have something they call, "The Principle of Sharing."

The Principle of Sharing was conceived out of a desire for oneness, a call to transparency, and a longing for strong love. It is based on the idea that if your spouse loves something, there must be something to love about it. So, they would read books together, teach each other things, and share everything they could, all in an effort to become one and understand each other fully.

One of the defining characteristics of love is the desire for union. We loved *The Principle of Sharing* because we found sharing to be rooted in a longing for oneness. *The Principle of Sharing* is the idea that *togetherness* in all things strengthens the bond of marriage and deepens the intimacy of love. For example, if your husband likes soccer (I love soccer!), be willing to put effort into understanding the game and watching along with him. Likewise, if your wife loves something (Audrey loves barre3), give it a try. Believe it or not, I actually go to a few classes a week to support Auj, and understand her better (plus I get a killer burn on my glutes).

These examples might not apply or work for you, but the idea is to be *willing* to share in order to grow in *oneness*. There is something beautifully sacrificial about being willing to love something you wouldn't normally love, for the sake of the person you love. **What is something you could participate in or share this week, in order to understand and love your spouse better?**

– Jeremy

Calendar

_____ / / _____

Mon.	**Tue.**
Wed.	**Thur.**
Fri.	**Sat.**
Sun.	Other:

Notes

Navigator's

1. What brought you joy this week?

2. What is something that was hard this week?

3. What is one specific thing I can do for you this week?

4. Is there any unconfessed sin, conflict, or hurt that we need to resolve and/or seek forgiveness for?

5. What is a dream, craving, or desire that has been on the forefront of your mind?

6. How can I pray for you this week?

Truth

The world gives us many reasons to have a divided marriage, to have a broken marriage, and to have a bitter marriage. Satan's ambition is to make marriage seem dispensable. He will do anything he can to steal, kill, and destroy it (John 10:10) I think one of the ways he does this is by planting festering lies in our minds. We begin to believe these lies as if they are truths, which leaves us feeling empty, disappointed, frustrated, and hurt.

Lies are like vicious weeds. If you don't pull them from the garden, they have the ability to overtake it. In order to keep the weeds from growing back, you have to pull them up by their roots. Metaphorically, the only way to stop the growth of lies is to replace them with truths.

If you are married, every day you have the power to kill the lies your spouse might be believing and replace them with ravishing truth. When you plant truth, it grows, transforms, and cultivates *more* truth.

Pull the lies and plant the truth in your marriage. Marriage is like a garden. If you don't yank the weeds, the fruitful plants will not be able to flourish. If you don't tend to the garden consistently, it will be much harder to tend to when you finally get around to it. Don't let your marriage be something that you finally get around to nurturing. Nurture your marriage with truth, and it will be a beautiful and blooming garden. Speak truth into your spouse's life - hard truth, honest truth, encouraging truth, affirming truth, and Biblical truth. Is there a hard truth you need to speak into your spouse's life in a loving way this week? Spend some time writing down or speaking truths about who your spouse is and who they are becoming!

"Truth without grace is surgery without anesthesia, but grace without truth is a bottle with no medicine in it." - Jimmy Evans

- Audrey

Calendar

_____ / / _____

Mon.	**Tue.**
Wed.	**Thur.**
Fri.	**Sat.**
Sun.	Other:

Notes

Navigators

1. What brought you joy this week?

2. What is something that was hard this week?

3. What is one specific thing I can do for you this week?

Council

4. Is there any unconfessed sin, conflict, or hurt that
    we need to resolve and/or seek forgiveness for?

5. What is a dream, craving, or desire that has been on the fore-
    front of your mind?

6. How can I pray for you this week?

Humility

"The reward of humility [that is, having a realistic view of one's importance] and the [reverent, worshipful] fear of the Lord Is riches, honor, and life." Proverbs 22:4 (AMP)

Humility is the breaking down of pride. Humility is the opposite of boastfulness, aggressiveness, and arrogance. Rather than, "Me first," humility allows us to say, "No, you first." Acting in humility says that you value and put others, specifically your spouse, above yourself.

"*True humility is not thinking less of yourself; it is thinking of yourself less.*" - C.S. Lewis

The bait of Satan is pride, the antonym to humility. Pride is precisely how he duped humanity in the first place. Then Jesus came and was the embodiment of humility, from His birth to His death (Luke 2:7; Luke 23). "*Sin came from the pride of Lucifer, and salvation came through the humility of Jesus.*" - Zac Poonen

"And what does the Lord require of you? To act justly and to love mercy and to walk humbly with your God." Micah 6:8 (NKJV) Are you walking humbly with God? **How can you think of yourself less, and your husband/wife more this week?**

- Jeremy

Calendar

_____ / ___ / _____

Mon.	**Tue**.
Wed.	**Thur**.
Fri.	**Sat**.
Sun.	Other:

Notes

_____
_____
_____
_____
_____
_____
_____
_____
_____

Navigators

1. What brought you joy this week?

2. What is something that was hard this week?

3. What is one specific thing I can do for you this week?

4. Is there any unconfessed sin, conflict, or hurt that we need to resolve and/or seek forgiveness for?

5. What is a dream, craving, or desire that has been on the fore-
   front of your mind?

6. How can I pray for you this week?

MONTHLY QUESTIONS

☐ How are we stewarding our finances?

☐ How is our sex life?

Sex

I don't know about you guys, but when we got married we had almost no idea what we were doing... I mean really, we were both virgins. On our honeymoon, we found ourselves feeling a whole gamut of emotions pertaining to sex. We felt passionate, turned on, awkward, frustrated, curious, insecure, unashamed, vulnerable, and in love. Do one or more these emotions resonate with your sex life?

We realized rather quickly that sex wasn't something we were going to master immediately... However, in order to learn how to better love each other sexually, we would need to *ask the hard questions, give honest answers, and be patient*. In an effort to help those who have experienced similar feelings in regards to their sex life, we have compiled a few questions to help you learn how to turn each other on, heat things up, and/or de-rut from a place of sexual complacency.

As you ask your spouse these intimate questions, be prepared to earnestly listen and honestly share. You may receive an unexpected answer, or an answer that is hard to hear. Even so, it's important not to judge your partner or show signs of disapproval. Let this be a time to share freely and learn! Also, <u>be specific</u> (that means you, husbands).

What are your beliefs about sex? How often do you want to have sex? Are you happy with our sex life right now? What turns you on? What can I do physically to show you how much I love you? Is our relationship physical enough for you? What would make it better? Is there something you are struggling with in regards to sex? How can we romance each other during the day? How do you show me that you are initiating sex? Is connecting emotionally before we have sex important to you? If so, how would you like to connect? How would you like to be held before, during, and after sex?

- Audrey

Calendar

_____ / / _____

Mon.	**Tue.**
Wed.	**Thur.**
Fri.	**Sat.**
Sun.	Other:

Notes
_____
_____
_____
_____
_____
_____
_____
_____
_____
_____

Navigators

1. What brought you joy this week?

2. What is something that was hard this week?

3. What is one specific thing I can do for you this week?

4. Is there any unconfessed sin, conflict, or hurt that we need to resolve and/or seek forgiveness for?

5. What is a dream, craving, or desire that has been on the forefront of your mind?

6. How can I pray for you this week?

Stewardship

The definition of stewardship is, "The responsible overseeing and protection of something considered worth caring for and preserving."

The fundamental Biblical principle of stewardship is that everything is the Lord's, and we are simply tasked with managing it well. Psalm 24:1 says, "The earth is the LORD's, and everything in it, the world, and all who live in it." (NIV)

C.S. Lewis puts it this way in *Mere Christianity*: "Every faculty you have, your power of thinking or of moving your limbs from moment to moment, is given you by God. If you devoted every moment of your whole life exclusively to His service, you could not give Him anything that was not in a sense His own already."

God gives us resources to be used, not hoarded. It is through giving that we gain. This sounds counterintuitive, as is to be expected with scripture, but it's true.

"'...Bring all the tithes into the storehouse so there will be enough food in my Temple. If you do,' says the LORD Almighty, 'I will open the windows of heaven for you. I will pour out a blessing so great you won't have enough room to take it in! Try it! Let me prove it to you!'" Malachi 3:10 (NLT)

What a beautiful challenge from the Lord! He wants us to prove that no object has control over our heart, and He wants us to loosen our grip on the things that provide a false sense of security. For where our treasure is, there our heart will be also (Matthew 6:21).

Are you being a good steward of what has been entrusted to you? What are some ways you can improve?

- Jeremy

Calendar

_____ / / _____

Mon.	**Tue.**
Wed.	**Thur.**
Fri.	**Sat.**
Sun.	Other:

Notes

Navigators

1. What brought you joy this week?

2. What is something that was hard this week?

3. What is one specific thing I can do for you this week?

Council

4. Is there any unconfessed sin, conflict, or hurt that we need to resolve and/or seek forgiveness for?

5. What is a dream, craving, or desire that has been on the forefront of your mind?

6. How can I pray for you this week?

Play

"The thief comes only in order to steal and kill and destroy. I came that they may have *and* enjoy life, and have it in abundance [to the full, till it overflows]." John 10:10 (AMP)

Don't be one of those married couples who stopped dating, stopped flirting, stopped laughing, and stopped playing after their wedding day… that's no fun! God desires for us to take delight (Psalm 37:4), embrace joy (Romans 15:13), and experience pleasure (Psalm 16:11). I know a lot of Christian, and non-Christian couples that make God out to be this disapproving, negative, rule maker. This bent way of viewing God deserves to be proven wrong. Our Lord wants us to laugh, play, enjoy, and delight! He created these things because He knew that they would be for our good. Yes, it's easy to get consumed with the tyranny of the urgent, the looming decisions, and the jam-packed schedules, but we can't let those things rob us of our playfulness, laughter, and having a little fun.

Remember when you were a child and your parents would schedule play dates for you? Sometimes I think that's what we need to do in our marriage: schedule a date with your spouse to just play, laugh, and enjoy doing something you love together. It can be something as simple as watching a movie, reading a book together, teaching each other something, cooking a meal, going for a drive and listening to music, taking a bath, or playing cards. Set some boundaries for your play date - money, issues with the kids, big decisions, dark pasts, and scheduling should be <u>off limits!</u> Don't believe the lie that tells you, you don't have time to play. You do! You just have to prioritize it like you would anything else (Ecclesiastes 3:2).

On the next page there is a calendar… Write down the words "PLAY DATE" under one of the days for next week! **Don't underestimate the power of playing together.**

- Audrey

Calendar

_____ / _____ / _____

Mon.	Tue.
Wed.	**Thur.**
Fri.	**Sat.**
Sun.	**Other:** Don't forget to schedule your play date!!!

Notes

_____

_____

_____

_____

_____

_____

_____

_____

_____

_____

Navigators

1. What brought you joy this week?

2. What is something that was hard this week?

3. What is one specific thing I can do for you this week?

4. Is there any unconfessed sin, conflict, or hurt that
    we need to resolve and/or seek forgiveness for?

5. What is a dream, craving, or desire that has been on the fore-
    front of your mind?

6. How can I pray for you this week?

Rhythm

Building healthy rhythms into our marriages is one of the most productive and preventative practices we can establish. Healthy rhythms become healthy habits, and healthy habits reap bountiful rewards.

Anyone who attempts something difficult, whether it be a diet, marathon, college degree, or a marriage, must first create healthy rhythms that work towards accomplishing their goal.

The next thing they do to accomplish their goal is to find a community or someone to do it with. Anyone who has tackled a diet before knows that it helps to have a partner for accountability and encouragement. It's proven to increase return on effort. Likewise, if you want to love your wife better or read your Bible more consistently, it helps to have a community that will hold you accountable.

Here are some ideas for healthy rhythms and habits that you can implement into your marriage: Navigator's Council, kiss goodnight every night, church every week, set a date night (weekly or monthly), pray together every day, turn your phones off at a certain time of the night, no phone zones, say thank you for the little things, speak daily words of encouragement, eat a meal together every day, or go to bed together.

This is not meant to be an exhaustive list; it's just to get you thinking about some habits to implement into your marriage. Circle a few that stand out to you, and/or write down your own on the next page!

Give this some serious thought – **What are some rhythms and habits that might be negatively affecting your marriage?**

"We are what we repeatedly do." - Aristotle

- Jeremy

Calendar

_____ / / _____

Mon.	Tue.
Wed.	**Thur.**
Fri.	**Sat.**
Sun.	Other:

Notes

_____

_____

_____

_____

_____

_____

_____

_____

_____

_____

_____

Navigators

1. What brought you joy this week?

2. What is something that was hard this week?

3. What is one specific thing I can do for you this week?

4. Is there any unconfessed sin, conflict, or hurt that we need to resolve and/or seek forgiveness for?

5. What is a dream, craving, or desire that has been on the forefront of your mind?

6. How can I pray for you this week?

MONTHLY QUESTIONS

☐ How are we stewarding our finances?

☐ How is our sex life?

Community

"Christian community is a web of stubbornly loyal relationships, in a complex and challenging situation who are committed to practicing the way of Jesus together for the renewal of the world." - Josh Tyvan

Community is more than just a group of friends. It's a group of people that you commit to doing life with, who have your best interest at heart, and who aren't afraid to share hard truth in love. Community is a group of people who consistently meet together (Hebrews 10:25). It's a group of people who want to be with Jesus, become like Jesus, and do what He did. *Church, wise council, accountability, and prayer* are all forms of community. We should seek out these things if we desire to have a Christ-centered thriving marriage that is *Beating50Percent.*

<u>Church</u> - Find a church and commit to it. No more of this "we are in between churches." Church should be your community, not just a place where you come and go. Your church community should encourage you, pray for you, push you towards Jesus, challenge you, and hold you accountable. The Bible talks about everyone being participators in church, not just spectators (1 Corinthians 14:26). Your gifts, skills, and personality should be missed when you're not there.

<u>Wise Council</u> – Think about an older wiser married couple that you admire. Ask if you can have dinner with them once a month!

<u>Accountability</u> – Invite it! Don't just receive all the encouragement that community has to offer, but get out of Dodge when they want to hold *you* accountable. Hand select a few couples or mentors to hold you accountable as individuals and as a couple.

<u>Prayer</u> – Ask people in your community to pray *for* and *with* you as a couple. Can you think of one other couple that you and your spouse could commit to praying for and asking prayer from? Create a group text for the four of you to share requests and text prayers!

- Audrey

Calendar

_____ / / _____

Mon.	Tue.
Wed.	**Thur.**
Fri.	**Sat.**
Sun.	Other:

Notes

_____

_____
_____
_____
_____
_____
_____
_____
_____
_____

Navigators

1. What brought you joy this week?

2. What is something that was hard this week?

3. What is one specific thing I can do for you this week?

4. Is there any unconfessed sin, conflict, or hurt that we need to resolve and/or seek forgiveness for?

5. What is a dream, craving, or desire that has been on the forefront of your mind?

6. How can I pray for you this week?

Romance

Romance is the continual effort to desire your spouse. It's the byproduct of pursuit.

Men, if you can relate, there are times when I just don't feel like romancing my wife. It's nothing against her, and it's *not* that I'm not attracted to her, I just get lazy... Anyone?

Seth Godin puts it this way, *"Do what you should do, and your mood will follow."* The whole idea is that if we know we should do something but don't feel like it, just do it anyway and through your actions your heart will change. It is by doing, that we change our feelings. We need to man-up and pursue our deepest desires over our strongest desires. Sometimes our strongest desire in the moment is to be lazy and scroll through our social media when our deepest desire is that our wife feels loved, pursued, and romanced.

Our wives need to be romanced and feel pursued. I'll be the first to say, "Man, is it hard...," but I will also be the first to say it has amazing effects on her life and our marriage.

I've heard it said, "You can judge the quality of a man by the smile on his wife's face."

Does your wife go to work feeling like she is treasured, romanced, and loved? Her attitude and smile will prove yes or no.

Women *need* to be romanced; it's in the fabric of their DNA.

If you don't know where to start, take the Love Language test as a starting point **www.5lovelanguages.com**. Be creative and specific in how you love your spouse based on their love language.

– Jeremy

Calendar

_____ / _____ / _____

Mon.	Tue.
Wed.	**Thur.**
Fri.	**Sat.**
Sun.	**Other:**
	Take the love language test this week, and write down some notes on your love languages below.

Notes
_____
_____
_____
_____
_____
_____
_____
_____
_____
_____
_____

Navigators

1. What brought you joy this week?

2. What is something that was hard this week?

3. What is one specific thing I can do for you this week?

4. Is there any unconfessed sin, conflict, or hurt that we need to resolve and/or seek forgiveness for?

5. What is a dream, craving, or desire that has been on the forefront of your mind?

6. How can I pray for you this week?

Patience

For our first married Christmas, Jeremy got me tickets to Disneyland. I quickly realized it was one of my favorite places on earth, and I remember thinking... "What if God designed us to live our whole life like we do when we're in Disneyland? To the full, with wide-eyed wonder, fearless, joy-filled, exploring, conquering, patient, laughing, shameless, in community, and squeezing His hand tightly through the ups and downs."

As Jeremy and I raced around Disneyland with our Fastpasses, I wished that there could be a Fastpass for life. But the moment the thought crossed my mind, I sensed the Lord saying to me, "There's no such thing as a 'Fastpass' for life Audrey." Then I was reminded of Romans 12:12 which says, "Be joyful in hope, patient in affliction, *faithful in prayer.*" (NIV) It got me thinking... how often have I missed a "ride" in my own life because I wasn't willing to *patiently wait,* or because I was looking for a Fastpass to no avail? There have been many times where I have impatiently waited for Jeremy to change, break a habit or start a new one. Instead of praying for God to change his heart (and then waiting *patiently*), I wanted to do the changing. Can somebody relate?! Have you ever wished you could just hand your spouse a Fastpass for something they are growing in, working on, or trying to change? **Are there frustrations in your marriage that you have been impatient about? Is there something you and your spouse are impatiently waiting for?**

Join us in replacing impatient frustration with prayer. Join us in waiting in line, rather than looking for a Fastpass. And join us in trusting that the Lord's timing is perfect (Psalm 18:30, Acts 1:7 Ecclesiastes 3:11 Psalm 27:14). On the note section of the next page, write down a few things that you are patiently and prayerfully waiting for together. "But if we hope for what we do not yet have, we wait for it patiently." Romans 8:25 (NIV)

- Audrey

Calendar

_____ / / _____

Mon.	Tue.
Wed.	**Thur.**
Fri.	**Sat.**
Sun.	Other:

Notes

_____

_____
_____
_____
_____
_____
_____
_____
_____
_____

Navigators

1. What brought you joy this week?

2. What is something that was hard this week?

3. What is one specific thing I can do for you this week?

Council

4. Is there any unconfessed sin, conflict, or hurt that we need to resolve and/or seek forgiveness for?

5. What is a dream, craving, or desire that has been on the fore-front of your mind?

6. How can I pray for you this week?

Teammate

A team is one or more people working toward achieving the same goal. A team does best when all of its teammates are healthy, respected, honored and valued. Your spouse needs to be treated as your teammate, not your opponent.

Viewing Audrey as my teammate was a perspective shift I made early on in our marriage thanks to Chris and Jamie Herb – our premarital counselors, good friends, and also the couple that inspired this journal! *"We are on the same team! We are not two opposing forces trying to negotiate a deal that benefits each party. No. We are partners, seeking the absolute best for our team. This way of thinking changes the way we operate and completely revolutionizes the game. It gives us freedom to disagree and 'battle it out' because there is trust that we are both for our team."* – Chris & Jamie Herb.

This teammate perspective within marriage has turned situations doomed for escalating conflict into healthy progressions of growth. We believe that the point of marriage is not marriage itself. Marriage is a vehicle in which we get to participate in something bigger, a grand plan by a mighty God. Your marriage should have a mission, a purpose that's bigger than itself. For Christ followers, that mission is reflecting the Gospel through your marriage, and if you have children, raising them up to be disciples of Christ. Beyond this, you might have a mission together that takes the form of a ministry, a business, or a social cause.

Next time you feel tempted to lash out at your spouse, retaliate, or react instead of respond, remind yourself that you're on the same team. The attack on your marriage is not your spouse; it's the fallen world we live in, the sin we are so easily entangled in, and the reality of the devil's schemes. Don't let bad sportsmanship "red card" your mission! **Remember, you're on the same team!**

– Jeremy

Calendar

_____ / / _____

Mon.	Tue.
Wed.	Thur.
Fri.	Sat.
Sun.	Other:

Notes

_____
_____
_____
_____
_____
_____
_____
_____
_____

Navigators

1. What brought you joy this week?

2. What is something that was hard this week?

3. What is one specific thing I can do for you this week?

4. Is there any unconfessed sin, conflict, or hurt that we need to resolve and/or seek forgiveness for?

5. What is a dream, craving, or desire that has been on the fore-front of your mind?

6. How can I pray for you this week?

MONTHLY QUESTIONS

☐ How are we stewarding our finances?

☐ How is our sex life?

Protect

It's much easier to protect your marriage than it is to put it back together. **To win a war, you have to know you're in one**. Every day, your marriage enters a battlefield. What are you doing to protect your marriage against the dangers of workaholism, anxiety, pride, stress, fear, loss, porn, addiction, comparison, social media, emotional cheating, that girl at the gym, in-laws, hormones, or idolizing your kids?

You're probably well aware of the attacks on your own marriage. As you read that list above, maybe you even began mentally adding to it. So, how the heck do we protect our marriages from this daily war?! How do we love our spouses faithfully, intentionally, specifically, creatively, and daily, in a world that seeks to prevent and destroy our efforts? **Through prayer**. Prayer is the armor that creates an impenetrable shield.

Read Ephesians 6:10-18 together. We believe that one of the greatest ways you can protect your marriage is through *prayer*! Fill in the blanks below with your spouse's name, and commit to praying this prayer of protection over him or her every day!

Father God, place on _____'s head the helmet of salvation to guard his/her thoughts and mind in Christ. Place on _____'s chest the breastplate of righteousness to guard his/her heart and keep it pure. Wrap around his/her waist the belt of truth to prevent any lies from creeping into his/her thoughts or heart, and keep him/her far from temptation. Put the sandals of peace on _____'s feet to keep him/her walking bravely and courageously without fear or worry. Give _____ the shield of faith to trust in your leading Lord, and the sword of the Spirit to fight against the fiery arrows of attack. Cover _____ with your full protection and armor as he/she enters the battlefield today. In Jesus name. Amen.

- Audrey

Calendar

_____ / / _____

Mon.	Tue.
Wed.	Thur.
Fri.	Sat.
Sun.	Other:

Notes

_____
_____
_____
_____
_____
_____
_____
_____
_____
_____

Navigators

1. What brought you joy this week?

2. What is something that was hard this week?

3. What is one specific thing I can do for you this week?

4. Is there any unconfessed sin, conflict, or hurt that we need to resolve and/or seek forgiveness for?

5. What is a dream, craving, or desire that has been on the fore- front of your mind?

6. How can I pray for you this week?

Integrity

One of the definitions of integrity is "the state of being whole and undivided." It relates perfectly to the oneness of marriage. In order to have an undivided marriage, we must have a marriage marked by integrity. This requires us to be honest with each other and honest with ourselves. Then marriage can do its refining work. Marriage has a way of shining a light on these areas of shady integrity. You are a person of integrity if you uphold a certain set of morals *no matter what*. In marriage, this means upholding the promise we made to love each other "no matter what." I never imagined that marriage would challenge my character so much. It is truly a refining experience as I am constantly seeing *reflections* of myself that need *reflection*.

Integrity is often not what people see, but it's who we really are. It's who we are when our spouse is not watching, it's who we are when we are on a business trip, at a work event, or attending a bachelor/bachelorette party. Integrity requires an unrelenting determination to stand for truth and stick to your standards, even when it's hard, hated, or a hassle. Let's subscribe to being men and women of integrity, people known for being reliable, trustworthy and honest, *even when no one is watching.*

"The integrity of the upright will guide them, But the crookedness of the treacherous will destroy them." Proverbs 11:3 (KJV)

This week's challenge is to recognize areas in your marriage where your integrity might be a little shady. Be honest with yourself, honest with God, and then honest with your spouse. Scripture tells us that it is far more rewarding to be poor with integrity, than rich and a fool. (Proverbs 19:1)

As Michael Jackson says, "*I'm starting with the man in the mirror. I'm asking him to change his ways.*"

- Jeremy

Calendar

_____ / / _____

Mon.	Tue.
Wed.	Thur.
Fri.	Sat.
Sun.	Other:

Notes

_____

_____

_____

_____

_____

_____

_____

_____

_____

_____

Navigators

1. What brought you joy this week?

2. What is something that was hard this week?

3. What is one specific thing I can do for you this week?

Council

4. Is there any unconfessed sin, conflict, or hurt that we need to resolve and/or seek forgiveness for?

5. What is a dream, craving, or desire that has been on the forefront of your mind?

6. How can I pray for you this week?

Reconcile

Seeking reconciliation requires both of you to hear each other out, forgive, and establish a solution that will bring peace. **Don't let proving a point become more important than resolving an issue.**

We hear people all the time saying things like, "compromise is key," in regards to their relationship. While the intentions of this statement are well meaning, we've found that compromise is only a quick and temporary fix. Compromise has been known to replace reconciliation. When you encounter arguments, strife, and disagreements in your marriage, the goal should be to seek _resolve_, rather than settle on a compromise. Seeking resolve requires more effort and time, but it is worth fighting for (pun intended). Compromises are prone to backfiring with bitterness and resentment, while solutions create win-win situations. And yes, it requires long conversations, patience, humility, prayer, and perseverance, but these things will reap the long term benefits for a marriage that stands unified - rather than divided. 2 Corinthians 5:18-19 says we have been given "the ministry of _reconciliation_." Our marriages should be marked by repentance, forgiveness, and _reconciliation_, not pride, animosity, and bitterness. Colossians 3:13 instructs us, "...be quick to forgive an offense. Forgive as quickly and completely as the Master forgave you." (MSG)

One thing that has really helped us be quick to forgive and reconcile is the physical act of holding hands. We've found that it's really hard to be mad at each other while holding hands. It's a silent act that says, "we're on the same team." Anytime Jer reaches over to grab my hand during a dispute, my heart is immediately softened, and my desire to be right is replaced with a desire to reconcile. Try this method, I think you'll be surprised how well it works.

- Audrey

Calendar

____ / / ____

Mon.	**Tue.**
Wed.	**Thur.**
Fri.	**Sat.**
Sun.	Other:

Notes

Navigators

1. What brought you joy this week?

2. What is something that was hard this week?

3. What is one specific thing I can do for you this week?

4. Is there any unconfessed sin, conflict, or hurt that we need to resolve and/or seek forgiveness for?

5. What is a dream, craving, or desire that has been on the forefront of your mind?

6. How can I pray for you this week?

Honesty

Honesty builds trust!

Being honest about everything will build a wall of trust and security around your marriage.

Honesty means there are no lies, no hiding, no sneaking around. You have nothing to hide, and because of that, your spouse trusts you. We build trust with our spouse through honesty.

Honesty is a "windows-open," no hiding philosophy. There is nothing better than the freedom that honesty offers.

"If you tell the truth, you don't need to remember anything." - Mark Twain

As our premarital counselor and good friend Chris Herb puts it, *"We are broken people living in a broken world. We are all vulnerable to choices that could hurt or end our marriage. I believe if we commit to leave nothing in the dark with our spouse and a few others, it can prevent several, if not most crises. Allowing others into our dark places of guilt, shame, and hurt brings freedom and gives us the upper-hand pursuing healing through our brokenness."*

I encourage you to be honest with your spouse! A windows-open, no-secrets philosophy sets a foundation for intimacy and closeness which can only be achieved through honesty.

Use question number four in this week's Navigator's Council to be honest about any darkness you might be hiding. **Momentary honesty might sting, but long term lies are infectious.**

- Jeremy

Calendar

_____ / / _____

Mon.	**Tue.**
Wed.	**Thur.**
Fri.	**Sat.**
Sun.	Other:

Notes

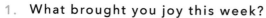
Navigators

1. What brought you joy this week?

2. What is something that was hard this week?

3. What is one specific thing I can do for you this week?

4. Is there any unconfessed sin, conflict, or hurt that we need to resolve and/or seek forgiveness for?

Council

5. What is a dream, craving, or desire that has been on the fore-front of your mind?

6. How can I pray for you this week?

MONTHLY QUESTIONS

☐ How are we stewarding our finances?

☐ How is our sex life?

Intimacy

God designed marriage to be the most intimate relationship that you experience in your life. It should be more intimate than your relationship with your best friend, your mom, your daughter, or dare I say… your smartphone. Aside from Christ, your spouse is the only person you "*become one*" with. And **oneness cannot be void of intimacy.**

We find intimacy through unconditional love, deep friendship, and sexual pleasure or romance. In order to deepen our intimacy in marriage, we must seek to love our spouse in all three ways: unconditionally, through friendship, and through sex.

Satan will do everything he can to steal, kill, and destroy your intimacy, so you must be willing to go to battle for it. You must be willing to seek out those intimate moments with your spouse in the face of all kinds of distractions, demands, and temptations. More intimacy leads to greater connection, and greater connection leads to a thriving marriage.

Think of one way you can deepen your intimacy with your spouse this week. For example, be open and honest about a struggle, pray together each morning, do something romantic, talk about what God's been teaching you lately, or commit to "making love" every night this week.

Choose **one specific way** that you are going to intentionally fight for intimacy with your spouse this week. Shake heads on it, and write it down in the notes section on the next page!

- Audrey

Calendar

_____ / / _____

Mon.	Tue.
Wed.	Thur.
Fri.	Sat.
Sun.	Other:

Notes

Navigators

1. What brought you joy this week?

2. What is something that was hard this week?

3. What is one specific thing I can do for you this week?

Council

4. Is there any unconfessed sin, conflict, or hurt that we need to resolve and/or seek forgiveness for?

5. What is a dream, craving, or desire that has been on the forefront of your mind?

6. How can I pray for you this week?

Vision

It was a Jimmy Evans podcast that blew my mind on the importance of having a vision in your marriage. The whole idea is that having a vision is having a *purpose*. It's having a reason to get up in the morning and it's working toward something. Having no vision can be frustrating and aimless.

Picture three ships at sea: the first ship has a crew with a vision to reach the Americas - that is their mission. So they wake up every morning eager to get to work. The second ship has no vision. They simply wake up, see which way the wind is blowing, and let what happens happen. They make no measurable progress because there is no vision to measure progress against. How do you know if you're being successful if you don't know what you're trying to accomplish? And then there's the third ship, the one with the undecided crew. Half of the crew wants to get to the Americas and the other half doesn't. You can imagine the conflict on that ship...

Having a vision is important for purpose, and agreeing on what that vision is, is just as vital. Every successful business, athlete, student, and sports team has a vision, so shouldn't our marriages? One reason many couples find themselves frustrated and confused is because they have no vision. There is confusion about the purpose and direction they're headed, so there is frustration because no measurable progress is being made.

The word "division" literally means having two separate visions... Fighting is typically initiated because of two separate visions. But when we have a collective vision we can rally around a goal, a mission, a vision. Spend some time this week discussing what your vision is.

"The heart of man plans his way, but the LORD establishes his steps." Proverbs 16:9 (ESV)

- Jeremy

Calendar

_____ / / _____

Mon.

Tue.

Wed.

Thur.

Fri.

Sat.

Sun.

Other:

Notes

Navigators

1. What brought you joy this week?

2. What is something that was hard this week?

3. What is one specific thing I can do for you this week?

Council

4. Is there any unconfessed sin, conflict, or hurt that we need to resolve and/or seek forgiveness for?

5. What is a dream, craving, or desire that has been on the fore-front of your mind?

6. How can I pray for you this week?

Connect

Navigator's Council has allowed Jeremy and I to *connect* with each other on a deeper level, and in new ways - this is one of its key benefits. Through the process of answering our Navigator's Council questions, we have learned how to increase our connection on a variety of levels. Feeling connected with Jeremy has lead to intimacy, security, trust, honesty, joy, and better communication in our marriage. Connecting with your spouse is vital to a prosperous marriage.

We've found that connecting in the little ways throughout the week has helped us feel connected in the hard times, big decisions, or when crisis hits. Here are some ideas for connecting with your spouse: **Physically** - a quick shoulder rub, hugs, kisses, or hold hands; **Emotionally** - nostalgia, relive a memory, looking through old photos, or watching a movie; **Intellectually** - watch a documentary, listen to a podcast, read a book, study a topic; **Spiritually** - pray together, read scripture together, sing worship songs together, listen to a sermon or podcast together, or do a devotional together; **Sexually** - flirt, romance, try something new, go to bed early; **Listening** - share a struggle, tell a story, ask questions, offer encouragement or advice; **Humor** - laugh at each other, do something that will make you laugh at each other, listen to/watch a comedy, play a game; **Hobbies** - Learn how to do something new together, root for the same sports team, work out together, cook together, teach each other something.

Did any of these ideas stand out to you? **Which level of connection (physical, emotional, intellectual) do you feel is most lacking in your marriage?** Do your actions prove that you desire a deeper connection with your husband/wife, or a stronger connection with your iPhone? How are you going to take a step towards connecting on a deeper level with your spouse this week?

– Audrey

Calendar

_____ / / _____

Mon.	**Tue.**
Wed.	**Thur.**
Fri.	**Sat.**
Sun.	Other:

Notes

Navigators

1. What brought you joy this week?

2. What is something that was hard this week?

3. What is one specific thing I can do for you this week?

4. Is there any unconfessed sin, conflict, or hurt that we need to resolve and/or seek forgiveness for?

5. What is a dream, craving, or desire that has been on the forefront of your mind?

6. How can I pray for you this week?

Spontaneity

Okay, for all the talk we've done about the commitments, purposes, and priorities, which have immense value, I feel it's necessary to add this topic in the journal. *Spontaneity.*

Commitments and priorities reap bountiful rewards, but they can also fizzle the spark in your marriage. Every once in awhile do something completely random and maybe even out of character, break up the routine and feel like you're in a movie.

Auj has been trying to get me to take a dance lesson with her. I have successfully evaded this horrible sounding experience. However, I've been thinking about it, and I've been inspired. It would be totally random and spontaneous. It's guaranteed to break up the rhythm of our usual outings and give her a good laugh.

Get some ideas from our #weekendidos hashtag on Instagram. For those that don't know what that is; every weekend we ask couples from around the world to hashtag their dates nights, life events, and activities with "**#weekendidos**." This has created a collection of fun ideas to scroll through in case you are looking for some spontaneity!

Use question number five this week in your Navigator's Council to plan something spontaneous with your spouse.

– Jeremy

Calendar

_____ / / _____

Mon.	**Tue**.
Wed.	**Thur**.
Fri.	**Sat**.
Sun.	Other:

Notes _____

_____
_____
_____
_____
_____
_____
_____
_____
_____

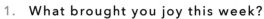

Navigator's

1. What brought you joy this week?

2. What is something that was hard this week?

3. What is one specific thing I can do for you this week?

4. Is there any unconfessed sin, conflict, or hurt that we need to resolve and/or seek forgiveness for?

Council

5. What is a dream, craving, or desire that has been on the fore-front of your mind?

6. How can I pray for you this week?

MONTHLY QUESTIONS

☐ How are we stewarding our finances?

☐ How is our sex life?

Appreciate

When was the last time you thanked your spouse?

Do you make your spouse feel appreciated? Do you feel appreciated?

"Give thanks in all circumstances; for this is the will of God in Christ Jesus for you." 1 Thessalonians 5:18 (ESV)

Do you find yourself giving thanks in all circumstances, or are you prone to complaining, grumbling, or criticizing?

Thankfulness often gets neglected in the midst of scheduling, to-do lists, decisions, and the day-today, but expressing your thankfulness to your spouse is a simple way to love him/her.

Thank your spouse for something mundane that they do for you daily that might go unnoticed (laundry, dishes, bathrooms, cooking, giving kids rides, managing the budget, etc.).

Take a moment to do this now.

<u>Your challenge for this week:</u> tell your spouse *every day* one reason you are thankful for them. This can be done through notes, texts, or verbally communicated face to face!

A person who feels appreciated will always do more than expected.

"Let the peace of Christ rule in your hearts, since as members of one body you were called to peace. And be thankful." Colossians 3:15 (NLT)

- Audrey

Calendar

_____ / / _____

Mon.	**Tue**.
Wed.	**Thur**.
Fri.	**Sat**.
Sun.	Other:

Notes

Navigators

1. What brought you joy this week?

2. What is something that was hard this week?

3. What is one specific thing I can do for you this week?

4. Is there any unconfessed sin, conflict, or hurt that we need to resolve and/or seek forgiveness for?

5. What is a dream, craving, or desire that has been on the fore-front of your mind?

6. How can I pray for you this week?

Hope

"May the God of hope fill you with all joy and peace in believing [through the experience of your faith] that by the power of the Holy Spirit you will abound in hope *and* overflow with confidence in His promises." Romans 15:13 (AMP)

Hope is not wishful thinking. No, hope is reliant. Hope is the fuel of persistence as we work towards a certain outcome. We have every reason to hope because of Christ's promises. Hope is an unwavering confidence and expectancy of the unknown and unseen. Without hope, we are prone to pessimism and fear. Without hope, we are confined to our natural human limitations. Without hope, our marriages might seem "unfixable." But because of Christ, we have every reason to hope, *no matter our circumstances.*

1 Peter 1:3 says that we have a "living hope through the resurrection of Jesus." This new LIVING HOPE that we have in Christ gives us access to the unlimited and far surpassing power and strength that is available to us through Christ. This living hope is Christ in us, with us, and going before us. Because Christ is in your marriage, with your marriage, and going before your marriage, *there is hope.* Even though our marriages are greatly susceptible to winds, waves, and storms, if we place our hope in Christ, we can trust wholeheartedly that our anchor will hold. Christ as our hope and anchor will keep us steady, afloat, and headed towards heavens harbor (Hebrews 6:19). "Let us hold unswervingly to the hope we profess, for he who promised is faithful." Hebrews 10:23

There is *always* hope because there is *always* God.

"*The whole world is going to be redeemed. Jesus is going to redeem spirit and body, reason and emotion, people and nature. There is no part of reality for which there is no hope.*" – Timothy Keller

– Audrey

Calendar

_____ / / _____

Mon.	**Tue.**
Wed.	**Thur.**
Fri.	**Sat.**
Sun.	Other:

Notes

_____

_____

_____

_____

_____

_____

_____

_____

_____

_____

Navigators

1. What brought you joy this week?

2. What is something that was hard this week?

3. What is one specific thing I can do for you this week?

4. Is there any unconfessed sin, conflict, or hurt that we need to resolve and/or seek forgiveness for?

5. What is a dream, craving, or desire that has been on the fore-front of your mind?

6. How can I pray for you this week?

Honor

Read 1 Peter 3:1 and 7 <u>together</u>. To honor your spouse is a verb. According to the dictionary, it means to "*regard with great respect or to fulfill an obligation or keep an agreement.*" The Bible talks a lot about honor. We are told to honor our parents (Ephesians 6:2), honor the Lord (1 Timothy 1:17), honor each other (Philippians 2:29), honor the Sabbath (Isaiah 58:13), honor our bodies (1 Thessalonians 4:4), honor our elders (1 Timothy 5:17), and finally, to honor our marriage (Hebrews 13:4; 1 Peter 3:7; Proverbs 12:4; Ephesians 5:33).

Hebrews 13:4 says, "Let marriage be held in honor among all." (ESV) Therefore, if we are told to honor our marriage, this means that we are to *regard our husbands and wives with great respect and keep our agreement* (aka remain faithful to our vows). To honor our husbands and wives is to recognize their worth and to treat them in a way that is a reflection of their immense value. We do this by cherishing them, encouraging them, praising them, respecting them, speaking highly of them, sacrificing for them, thanking them, and protecting them.

Proverbs 12:4 says, "An excellent wife is the crown of her husband." (ESV) Wives, are you your husband's crown? Are you the token of his honor? Husbands, do you treat your wife as your crowning glory? Is she highly treasured, protected, and beautifully portrayed by you? Are you proud to show her off and eager to lift her up?

On the contrary, comparison will <u>*dishonor*</u> your spouse. Comparison robs your husband or wife of honor, value, respect, and creates self-consciousness and insecurity. In comparing, you might not be aiming to devalue, disrespect, or dishonor your spouse, but they will feel that way. Don't let comparison blind you to the beautiful, Godly, respectful, and worthy man or woman that God has given you. **Let's be women who honor our husbands with respect and men who honor our wives with love** (Ephesians 5:33).

- Audrey

Calendar

_____ / / _____

Mon.	**Tue.**
Wed.	**Thur.**
Fri.	**Sat.**
Sun.	Other:

Notes

Navigators

1. What brought you joy this week?

2. What is something that was hard this week?

3. What is one specific thing I can do for you this week?

4. Is there any unconfessed sin, conflict, or hurt that we need to resolve and/or seek forgiveness for?

5. What is a dream, craving, or desire that has been on the fore-front of your mind?

6. How can I pray for you this week?

Change

One of my promises to Audrey on our wedding day was, "Audrey, I promise to pursue the *new you*, every year…"

One thing I vowed to do was acknowledge that the Audrey I married might not be the same Audrey as the years go by.

I met a mysterious, adventurous tomboy, fell in love with a Godly, aspiring country girl, proposed to a 23-year-old collegiate runner, married a beautiful writer, spent a year with a hard-working corporate sales lady, then started a business with a 25-year-old entrepreneur, barre3 teacher, and wise woman on a mission.

Audrey has changed and matured a lot over the seven years that I've know her, and I expect this to continue. Embracing change has me excited for all the different versions of my wife that I get to be married to. Change is natural, constant, and inevitable.

We can't avoid change, so we must understand that in order to achieve the goals we have set for our marriages, we need to be *proactively* changing and accepting of change. The thing is, marriage *requires* change. In marriage, we are constantly being escorted into a selfless life for the renewal and experience of the Kingdom of God.

Change has the ability to speed up the process of maturity *if we let it*. It has the ability to push us towards our potential. Let's be constantly learning how to love the beautiful, ever-changing versions of our husbands and wives year after year.

– Jeremy

Calendar

_____ / / _____

Mon.	**Tue.**
Wed.	**Thur.**
Fri.	**Sat.**
Sun.	**Other:**

Notes

_____

_____

_____

_____

_____

_____

_____

_____

_____

_____

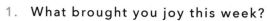

Navigator's

1. What brought you joy this week?

2. What is something that was hard this week?

3. What is one specific thing I can do for you this week?

4. Is there any unconfessed sin, conflict, or hurt that we need to resolve and/or seek forgiveness for?

Council

5. What is a dream, craving, or desire that has been on the forefront of your mind?

6. How can I pray for you this week?

MONTHLY QUESTIONS

☐ How are we stewarding our finances?

☐ How is our sex life?

Expectations

Expectations hold immense power. They are the assumed sum of our desires. When we don't manage our expectations, we buy into the lie that our husbands and wives are responsible for meeting all of our wants and needs and that they should automatically know exactly how to do that. Sounds silly, but both Jeremy and I have been guilty of this in our relationship. If you've been married for any length of time, you have likely experienced the disappointment associated with unmanaged expectations. You know... those moments when what *actually* happened was different than what was you thought was *supposed* to happen (your ideals that were not communicated).

If we are not articulating our expectations, then we can't justify being bitter, frustrated, or angry if they are not met. I know for most women, myself included, this is especially convicting. Here are a few strategies that have helped us develop healthy expectation management:

Communicate your hopes, wants, and needs - For example, whenever Jeremy and I are on our way to an event, we take a moment to ask the other, "What are your expectations for this?" This question helps us establish what each of our hopes, wants, and needs are for that circumstance.

Be clear before birthdays, anniversaries, and holidays - You *need* to be clear about what your birthday, anniversary, Christmas, etc. expectations are.

Discuss unmet expectations and praise met ones - *A person who feels appreciated will always do more than expected.*

Do you have any expectations that you have not communicated?

- Audrey

Calendar

_____ / / _____

Mon.	**Tue.**
Wed.	**Thur.**
Fri.	**Sat.**
Sun.	Other:

Notes

Navigators

1. What brought you joy this week?

2. What is something that was hard this week?

3. What is one specific thing I can do for you this week?

4. Is there any unconfessed sin, conflict, or hurt that
   we need to resolve and/or seek forgiveness for?

5. What is a dream, craving, or desire that has been on the fore-
   front of your mind?

6. How can I pray for you this week?

Conflict

The path to becoming one isn't always easy. As we mentioned earlier, it is both a truth about your marriage and something you get to live out. However, we all come from very different backgrounds, upbringings, parenting, spending habits, theologies, so we are bound to have conflict. It's not a matter of *if* you will fight but *when*. So, if we know conflict is inevitable, *how do we fight fair* with parameters that are *healthy* and *productive*, rather than *harmful* and *destructive*?

Here are our techniques for fighting fair:

Don't fight in public - Seriously, <u>don't</u>. Fighting in public usually escalates the fight. Both people become self-conscious about how the fight looks to family, friends, or strangers which makes the situation more about the fight and less above resolving the issue.

Cooling off periods to avoid yelling, interrupting, or retaliation -*The volume of your voice does not increase the validity of your argument.*

Eliminate "always" and "never" - These types of accusations will only lead your spouse to focus on defending *themselves*, instead of seeking to understand *you*.

Don't drink. For obvious reasons… it just doesn't promote an enviorment for resolution.

Don't vent to your mom, best friend, OR Facebook - The motive behind this is likely drama. If you are truly seeking to resolve an issue in your marriage, this will only be a hindrance to your efforts and break the barrier of trust and confidentiality.

Make your own rules for conflict and fighting fair.

- Jeremy

Calendar

_____ / / _____

Mon.	Tue.
Wed.	**Thur.**
Fri.	**Sat.**
Sun.	**Other:**
	Establish your rules for fighting fair, and write them down below.

Notes

_____

_____

_____

_____

_____

_____

_____

_____

_____

_____

Navigators

1. What brought you joy this week?

2. What is something that was hard this week?

3. What is one specific thing I can do for you this week?

4. Is there any unconfessed sin, conflict, or hurt that
    we need to resolve and/or seek forgiveness for?

5. What is a dream, craving, or desire that has been on the fore-
    front of your mind?

6. How can I pray for you this week?

Seek

To find and still seek, now that is love.

This statement beautifully illustrates the mission of *Beating50Percent.*

We hope to inspire couples to give *more* to their marriages over time, rather than falling into the rut of complacency. To keep seeking your husband or wife means to continue pursuing them, romancing them, serving them, encouraging them, and loving them *more* and *more.*

We need to keep seeking our spouses. We need to persistently pursue them, and relentlessly learn how to love them better. Our pursuit shouldn't end when we say, "I do." Our actions should give real meaning to that promise of commitment, each and every day after the wedding, with increasing intent. This is "staying I do." **#stayingido**

If we want to have better than average marriages, we need to view them as **never ending love stories.**

One of the beautiful aspects about marriage is that we don't have to impress our spouse (like when we were dating), but we *get* to impress our spouse by still seeking them every day.

Seek your spouse *more* with the years, not less.

-Audrey

Calendar

_____ / / _____

Mon.	**Tue.**
Wed.	**Thur.**
Fri.	**Sat.**
Sun.	Other:

Notes

Navigators

1. What brought you joy this week?

2. What is something that was hard this week?

3. What is one specific thing I can do for you this week?

Council

4. Is there any unconfessed sin, conflict, or hurt that we need to resolve and/or seek forgiveness for?

5. What is a dream, craving, or desire that has been on the forefront of your mind?

6. How can I pray for you this week?

Celebrate

Your marriage is worth celebrating beyond your wedding day.

Celebrating is an act of encouragement. It's a recognition that you have either achieved or accomplished something.

This goes back to encouragement and affirmation.

Audrey and I love celebrating, partly because we need it, and partly because it's fun. When we finish a project, one of us has a breakthrough with work, we get through a tough season, we move, etc,. we love going to the store and picking out a special bottle of wine, then we set aside a few hours in the evening to celebrate. It's fast, attainable, fun, and doesn't take a lot of planning. Sometimes it's full of conversation, sometimes it's just doing nothing. The point is that it is intentional, and we are recognizing the progression of our journey.

If it's our anniversary or a birthday, we try to do something a little more adventurous. We celebrate because it's fun, necessary, and rejuvenating. We know our marriage needs it, and we know yours does too.

There will be plenty of highs and lows in your marriage journey, so be sure to take time to *celebrate* the highs.

– Jeremy

Calendar

_____ / / _____

Mon.	**Tue**.
Wed.	**Thur**.
Fri.	**Sat**.
Sun.	Other:

Notes

Navigator's

1. What brought you joy this week?

2. What is something that was hard this week?

3. What is one specific thing I can do for you this week?

4. Is there any unconfessed sin, conflict, or hurt that we need to resolve and/or seek forgiveness for?

5. What is a dream, craving, or desire that has been on the fore-front of your mind?

6. How can I pray for you this week?

MONTHLY QUESTIONS

☐ How are we stewarding our finances?

☐ How is our sex life?

Friendship

There are three types of love that the Bible speaks of: *Eros*, *Agape*, and *Philos*. *Eros* love is what makes us fall in love, and *Agape* love is what makes us remain faithful to the commitment of marriage, but *Philos* love is the kind of love we need on a daily basis. Philos love is companionship love or deep friendship. Hardwired into our DNA is a longing for loyal and intimate friendship. I think that's why most people will say that they married their best friend. But we can't just marry our best friend, who we marry must remain our best friend, even after 5, 25, and 50 years of marriage. If our longing for intimate friendship is not being fulfilled by our spouse, we might end up looking for it from someone else…

John S. Gottman writes, in his book <u>The Seven Principles for Making Marriage Work</u>, "*Happily married couples aren't smarter or more beautiful than others, and they don't live in castles in the clouds where there's no conflict or negative feelings. They've simply learned to let their positive feelings about each other override their negative ones… They know each other deeply and enjoy being together. They do little things every day to stay connected and to show each other they care. In short, they are friends.*"

Like friends do, Jeremy and I share our struggles, ask advice, encourage one another, serve one another, and laugh with one another. I don't necessarily need Jeremy to remind me that he is going to be faithful to love me everyday (*Agape* love), and I don't necessarily need Jeremy to physically romance me everyday (*Eros* love), but I <u>do</u> need him to be my friend everyday (*Philos* love). And this highlights the importance of *Philos* love: it makes us feel loved on a day-to-day basis.

Don't let anything or anyone stand in the way of being your spouse's best friend.

- Audrey

Calendar

_____ / _____ / _____

Mon.	Tue.
Wed.	Thur.
Fri.	Sat.
Sun.	Other:

Notes

_____
_____
_____
_____
_____
_____
_____
_____
_____

Navigators

1. What brought you joy this week?

2. What is something that was hard this week?

3. What is one specific thing I can do for you this week?

Council

W_____/52

4. Is there any unconfessed sin, conflict, or hurt that we need to resolve and/or seek forgiveness for?

5. What is a dream, craving, or desire that has been on the forefront of your mind?

6. How can I pray for you this week?

Listen

"Understand this, my dear brothers and sisters: You must all be quick to listen, slow to speak, and slow to get angry. Human anger does not produce the righteousness God desires." – James 1:19-20 (NLT)

We all have built within us an innate desire to be heard, to be right, and to win. But God says it is better to listen, that we don't know it all, and that the last will be first in the Kingdom of God. Whoa…

Fight your battles on your knees and you will win every time.

Listening is different than hearing! Yes, communication is <u>vital</u>, but it doesn't matter unless it's met with listening ears! Discussions escalate into fights when nobody's listening and everybody's talking.

Audrey and I have had our worst disagreements when neither of us are listening. It's like we are both waiting for the other to take a breath so we can talk again, and we end up reacting instead of responding. You can only respond if you've listened. We can listen five times faster than we speak. So what are we doing with all that extra time? Are we constructing a genius dialogue that disregards all that they've said, or are we listening to understand?

Many of our arguments stem from Audrey feeling like she is not being heard. I hear her, but I don't listen. One trick we have implemented is the touch, stop, look technique. When I am doing something, it is very difficult for me to listen, and I know I'm not alone! Ok, I'm a guy. So when it is something important, Audrey knows that all I need is a touch of some kind (a hand on the shoulder) so that I can stop, look, then listen to what she is saying. This assures Audrey that I heard her, and it gives me a chance to respond.

- Jeremy

Calendar

_____ / ____ / _____

Mon.	Tue.

Wed.	Thur.

Fri.	Sat.

Sun.	Other:
	You've almost filled up your journal! Order your new Navigator's Council journal here: NavigatorsCouncil.com

Notes

_____

_____

_____

_____

_____

_____

_____

_____

_____

_____

Navigators

1. What brought you joy this week?

2. What is something that was hard this week?

3. What is one specific thing I can do for you this week?

Council

4. Is there any unconfessed sin, conflict, or hurt that we need to resolve and/or seek forgiveness for?

5. What is a dream, craving, or desire that has been on the forefront of your mind?

6. How can I pray for you this week?

Unique

Your marriage is *unique*, one of a kind, and a story that cannot be copied. God created each of you uniquely, and then He joined you together to make you an even greater representation of his magnificent creativity.

God is the author of your love story, and He doesn't write the same love story twice.

Stop comparing your love story to someone else's. Stop comparing your love story to the photos you see on Instagram. Stop comparing your love story to your parents'. Stop comparing your love story to Jeremy and me. Comparison will rob you of joy, thankfulness, peace, contentment, vision, and uniqueness. It's crippling. On top of that, social media has the power to make you constantly feel like your relationship is sub-par, unfulfilling, or even failing.

We must realize that every couple has a chapter in their story that they don't read out loud. Quit looking at other people's relationships and comparing them to yours. Refuse to let Hollywood set the standards for how your husband should love you. Stop coveting a better version of your spouse. And don't let yourself become bitter, disappointed, or resentful because your husband doesn't treat you exactly like you witnessed some other husband treat his wife.

Let God write your unique and beautiful love story. Ruthlessly eliminate comparison from your thoughts, heart, and marriage. You will experience the depths of *joy* if you choose to delight in what you have, rather than strive to obtain what you see. Your love story is beautiful, worthy, divine, intricate, unfolding, unique, and only yours. Embrace it, love it, and share it.

- Audrey

Calendar

_____ / / _____

Mon.	**Tue.**
Wed.	**Thur.**
Fri.	**Sat.**
Sun.	**Other:** This week, share your #3sentencelovestory

Notes

Navigators

1. What brought you joy this week?

2. What is something that was hard this week?

3. What is one specific thing I can do for you this week?

4. Is there any unconfessed sin, conflict, or hurt that
    we need to resolve and/or seek forgiveness for?

5. What is a dream, craving, or desire that has been on the fore-
    front of your mind?

6. How can I pray for you this week?

Reflection

"Every present moment has future implications" -Beth Moore
Reflection is studying *you*. Reflection is taking a pause... Selah.
Reflection provides perspective, and perspective is derived from history. When you reflect back on where you came from, you can increase your understanding of your standing.

We started **Navigator's Council** out of a desire for reflection to do its work by providing direction and stimulating growth. We hope Navigator's Council has been a beneficial tool for you to review where you've been and where you're headed. We hope it has helped you connect, communicate, and grow in love. We hope it has helped you honestly share and earnestly listen to one another. We hope it has offered insight on how you can love each other better and how you can live worthy of the calling you have received.

The aim of reflection is to study your own history and hopefully find value, understanding, and purpose that you can apply to your marriage. **You have now been doing Navigator's Council every week for ONE FULL YEAR!** We are fist pumping for you! Seriously, it's a hefty commitment, but we hope it has reaped abundance in your marriage.

This week, take some time to review your old Navigator's Council journal entries. Reflect on what you have learned about each other, areas you have grown in, hardships you have endured, accomplishments you have achieved, ways you have changed, prayers that have been answered, and reasons to be thankful.

We hope that as you spend some time reflecting together, the "man in the mirror" nods back at you in satisfaction... not because you see a mirror image, but because your reflection shows you a new one.

- Jeremy and Audrey

Calendar

_____ / ____ / _____

Mon.	**Tue.**
Wed.	**Thur.**
Fri.	**Sat.**
Sun.	**Other:** If this practice has had a positive impact on your marriage, don't keep it to yourself, share it with others. #NavigatorsCouncil

Notes
_____
_____
_____
_____
_____
_____
_____
_____
_____
_____

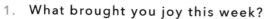

Navigators

1. What brought you joy this week?

2. What is something that was hard this week?

3. What is one specific thing I can do for you this week?

4. Is there any unconfessed sin, conflict, or hurt that we need to resolve and/or seek forgiveness for?

5. What is a dream, craving, or desire that has been on the fore-
   front of your mind?

6. How can I pray for you this week?

MONTHLY QUESTIONS

☐ How are we stewarding our finances?

☐ How is our sex life?

To find and

shits

seek

now that is love

Congratulations!

You have successfully completed a full year of Navigator's Council! High five!

If this has been something that has strengthened your communication, understanding, and love toward one another, then <u>don't stop now</u>!

We hope you continue this practice of communicating better, connecting deeper, and growing in love with your spouse.

Visit NavigatorsCouncil.com to get your new Navigator's Council journal!

———————————

Jeremy and Audrey currently live in Bend, Oregon. Together, they founded *Beating50Percent* - a marriage ministry, blog, and community. Jeremy is a photographer, videographer and part time farmer on his family's farm - Roloff Farms. Audrey is a barre3 instructer and runs a lifestyle blog called *AujPoj* where she has a clothing line and writes devotionals for women. They love camping, skiing, and exploring the Pacific Northwest.

WHERE TO FIND US ONLINE

@jeremyroloff
@audreyroloff
@beating50

Jeremy Roloff
Audrey Roloff
Beating50Percent

Jeremy & Audrey Roloff

@JeremyJRoloff
@AudreyMirabella
@Beating50

Jeremy Roloff
Audrey Roloff
Beating50Percent

JeremyRoloff.com
AujPoj.com
Beating50Percent.com